THE GREAT SHIP

THE GREAT SHIP

ERNLE BRADFORD

OPEN ROAD
INTEGRATED MEDIA
NEW YORK

Copyright © 1986 by Ernle Bradford

ISBN 978-1-4976-3789-4

This edition published in 2014 by Open Road Integrated Media, Inc.
345 Hudson Street
New York, NY 10014
www.openroadmedia.com

Foreword

The great ship no longer dominates the high seas of the world. Her end came in World War II when, first at Taranto in 1940 and secondly at Pearl Harbour in 1941, the power of the carrier-borne aircraft over the battleship was conclusively demonstrated. The era of the ship of the line, the battleship, was over and, although both the Americans and the Japanese deployed superb battleships in the war in the Pacific, there was never any engagement of the nature for which they had been designed. The aircraft carrier was the decisive arm in all the great actions. Although one or two battleships have still remained in commission in the United States navy, and have been used on occasions as bombardment vessels against gun positions and troop concentrations ashore, the story of the great ship is concluded.

During its long reign, from the sixteenth to the mid-twentieth century, it was the most powerful individual weapon of war in the world. Strategically, it determined the outcome of wars; tactically, it dominated sea battles. It protected or destroyed ports and harbour installations, and prevented the concentration of troops at selected points on the shore. Where the supreme warship moved there was peace or war, and territories safeguarded, or invaded and conquered. Although the aircraft carrier became the dominant ship during World War II, it was not the vessel itself but the aircraft that it carried that were the important factors. Now that the aircraft carrier itself, on account of its high vulnerability in modern warfare, is threatened with extinction the era of the great ship has assumed its place in history. It is a colourful and grand, as well as an exciting place, for these ships were not only imposing but often beautiful objects in themselves. They were subjects for painters from their earliest days (and later for photographers) just as much as if they had been supreme examples of architecture ashore. The nuclear submarine, which now dominates not only the sea but the cities of the world, is as functional looking as a cigar case. Furthermore it suffers from the terrifying disadvantage that its strength can only be displayed by an action that unleashes a holocaust. The great ship by its very presence, visible to other ships as well as towns and coastlines, could remind people of who exercised power without necessarily having to prove it. In the course of this function power could be seen allied with beauty. Unlike the flash of a plane in the sky or the whale back of a submarine glimpsed by chance, it was the deliberate presentation of these two very different qualities, held within one image, that carried the message.

The term is first found in the fifteenth century when '*great ships*, carracks, ships, barges and ballingers' are listed in the fleet of Henry V of England. It meant little more at that time than a large cargo carrier, adapted for fighting with 'castles' added fore and aft, and designed for carrying men, horses and stores across the Channel during the Anglo-French wars. If an action did occur at sea it was fought by boarding parties, using the castles as points of offence and defence. Archers supplied the fire power during the run in to close with the enemy. Great sea endurance — the ability to withstand winds and weather as well as the capacity to carry provisions and war materials for a considerable length of time — was not yet a requirement. It was the arrival of the gun at sea that transformed naval actions, just as the siege gun ashore had already changed land warfare and begun to render castles and fortified townships redundant. Ship-based artillery was first used in the Mediterranean aboard the oar-propelled galley, sail-and-oar galleasses, and then galleons. The arrival of the gun in the all-sail ship on the oceans of the world transformed everything for ever.

My object is not to provide yet another history of battleships, but to trace from its beginnings the evolution of this magnificent fighting vessel over the centuries, selecting one or two ships from each period and illustrating their use in action. The individual ships are often no more than representative of their types — common enough perhaps in their age — but the actions with which they became associated are often ones which opened whole eras of history. A very few, such as *Victory,* and now *Mary Rose,* have been preserved but most have gone along with the men who sailed and fought them. Highly regarded in their time for what they represented, they are now commemorated in records and histories, and above all in paintings and drawings, where they can be seen in the glory that once was theirs.

CHAPTER ONE

Distant Gunfire

It was September 1538 and a fleet of over a hundred galleys of Suleiman I, Sultan of Turkey, was off the south coast of Crete harrying the coastline and carrying off young men for service on the oar benches. The Sultan and the Republic of Venice were at war, and all Venetian territories — such as Crete — were therefore subject to attack. As Venice was a sea power, the Sultan had recently expanded his navy until he had more ships than almost any other power in the Mediterranean. They were commanded by his high admiral, Kheir-ed-Din, known to Europeans as Barbarossa, Red Beard, the greatest Mediterranean seaman of his time and one of the enduring names in the long naval history of that sea. His objective in this sweep south from Constantinople through the Aegean was not only to collect galley slaves and tribute from former Venetian territories, but to break the sea power of the Christian kingdoms if he could, thus securing a safe passage for his master's army into Europe. Italy was the prime target and the Turks, although proving themselves victorious at sea the year before, had failed to land forces at Brindisi. Barbarossa knew that an alliance of Christian powers was gathering up north in the Adriatic with the object of destroying the new Turkish navy once and for all.

The war vessel in the Mediterranean at this time was still the oared galley which had been dominant in these tideless and — in the summer months — often windless waters over all the centuries. Changing only slightly in form since the days of the Greeks and Romans, the galley's method of attack was to use its long beaked ram to damage the enemy, this action being followed by boarding parties. The major change in recent years had been the arrival of the gun at sea and, since galleys were necessarily of light-weight construction, only small guns could be adapted for naval warfare. These were mounted on reinforced platforms in the bows, but the main work was still done by the ram. Similar light guns might be mounted in the stern, as well as lighter ones still attached to the rails. Nearly all ships by this time had adopted the centre-line rudder in place of the steering paddle or paddles of antiquity (though the side rudder could still be seen as late as 1500), and in the Mediterranean all were carvel built.

The great distinction between the ships of the Mediterranean and those of northern Europe lay in the basic method of constructing the hull. Mediterranean ships, as far back as classical times, had been carvel built, that is to say each plank butted up against the plank above and the one below it. In the north, on the other hand, clinker building was the general rule: here the external planks overlapped downwards and were fastened with a clinch or nail. (The English word 'carvel' derives from the caravel, a fast, light ship of Spanish and Portuguese origin, thus confirming the word's southern derivation.) Apart from the fact that carvel building was stronger, it had another attractive feature for shipwrights when the age of the gun arrived — it presented a smooth external surface. In a clincher-built vessel, with its overlapping planks, it was difficult to cut gun ports, especially with lids fitting closely to them, and northern ships, in the transition period, are often seen to have been rebuilt from clinker to carvel so as to accommodate the new gun ports. The Venetians, who had a considerable trade with the countries of northern Europe, had long observed that the Mediterranean galley was quite unsuitable in those windy and tide-swept seas; its light construction, low freeboard and exposed oar ports making it dangerously unsafe.

Unwilling to forego the oars which were so essential to the Mediterranean, but realizing the necessity for sails in northern waters, their answer was compromise: the galleasse or sail- and oar-propelled galleon. Venetian galleasses of this type traded regularly with England, where their size and construction were naturally noted by native shipwrights. (The Anthony Anthony illustrated roll of ships in the navy of Henry VIII in 1545 shows English galleasses clearly built on Venetian lines.) At the same time, bearing in mind their northern trading routes, the Venetians followed by the Genoese and others even began experimenting with straightforward sailing ships — although like all sailing vessels of the period they always had aboard a number of large sweeps for manhandling the ship in harbour or helping her in a calm. This type of vessel was known as the carrack: a large, full-rigged ship, and the original 'great ship' as it became known in the north.

Barbarossa, as he was casually harrying the southern coast of Crete, received word that the combined fleets of Venice, Genoa and the Pope, under the overall command of Andrea Doria, admiral of the Emperor Charles V, were at sea. The fast galleot that brought this message informed him that the fleet had been sighted in the Adriatic, heading south towards the Ionian islands. Part of the Venetian empire, already threatened by Barbarossa in the previous year, the Ionian islands were obviously menaced by his recent foray and it was clear to the Sultan's admiral that his gage of battle — as he had always intended — was being accepted by the Christian powers.

The battle of Preveza which was to follow was a triumph for Barbarossa while Andrea Doria never recovered from the disgrace. The battle remains of interest for it is one of the first occasions on record where the gun power and the strength of an all-sail vessel showed that the days of the galley were numbered. It foreshadowed the whole future of seapower in Europe for centuries to come.

Preveza was a Turkish village standing at the entrance to the narrow channel that leads into the Gulf of Arta on the west coast of Greece, north of the Gulf of Patras and slightly north again of the island of Levkas. On the south side of the channel across from Preveza itself was Aktion Point,

better known in former times as Actium where Anthony
and Cleopatra had been decisively defeated by Octavius.
While Barbarossa began the long haul north across the late
summer sea, the allied fleets were very slowly assembling.
In these days of oars and lateen sails (for use when the
wind was slack) one of the most difficult parts of any such
operation was to get all the ships together in one place and
at one time. Communications were inevitably poor, almost
nonexistent once the ships had left their home ports, and
it was not until mid-September that the allied fleet was at
last assembled in Corfu roads. And still they waited before
proceeding south to seek the Sultan's fleet for an addition
to their own, a further fifty large sailing ships or 'galleons'
whose firepower, it was believed, would turn the tables on
the enemy and break Turkish sea power once and for all.

Unfortunately, as was to be seen on this occasion, mixed
fleets of oared galleys and sailing ships could never work
happily together. The weather which suited the one did not
suit the other, while the long delay caused by waiting for
the sailing ships detained by Mediterranean calms caused
the fleet under Andrea Doria to allow the Sultan's admiral
to make a decisive move ahead of them and take his ships
up Preveza Strait and into the Gulf of Arta. Once here, from
the security of the anchorage, and protected as it was by
Turkish guns in Preveza itself, he could sally out and harass
the enemy as and when it suited him. It was not until 25
September that the complete allied fleet had assembled at
Corfu and Andrea Doria, taking advantage of a favourable
northerly wind, managed to bring his awkward combination
of sail and oared vessels down together to blockade Preveza.
In numbers he now far exceeded the enemy, and in the
additional firepower provided by the galleons he had more
guns than there were in the whole of the Turkish fleet.

It is a curious fact of history that the heavily-gunned ship
should first be heard of in action against troops ashore, and
that what must surely be one of the last such actions of a
battleship in the second half of the twentieth century should
be in similar circumstances. When in 1984 the USS *New*

Jersey, a battleship from the World War II, opened fire with her great guns on troops and gun positions off Beirut, she was repeating the action that had first been heralded at Preveza — the use of massive firepower from the sea against enemy troops in otherwise unassailable positions. For in 1538 the Turks, fearful that the fleet investing Preveza might land troops and seize the comparatively weak fort, thus trapping the Turkish fleet within the Gulf of Arta, despatched soldiers to Preveza where they began entrenching themselves along the shoreline. Their action was sensible enough, especially since some of the officers with Andrea Doria were urging him to allow them to do just what had been expected of them.

Doria's reason for not complying was that in the third week of September, saddled with a large composite fleet, he was rightly fearful of having his ships caught on a lee shore held by the enemy. If that happened, he would be compelled to sail away and abandon the men who had landed. From mid-September onwards, as Doria knew well from a lifetime's experience, the Mediterranean is liable to become stormy. Barbarossa knew this too, which was one of his reasons for hastening with his galleys into the sheltered gulf. A gale from the north, always possible in that area of the sea, would hurl Doria's ships down onto the north coast of Levkas island, while a westerly would drive him onto Preveza itself. As it was, the Turks having made the first move, he needed to do nothing but resort to the firepower of his fleet. It was this that Barbarossa had been fearful of when he had urged his own commanders not to advance troops within range of the allied fleet. He himself had never encountered the cannon fire of galleons, although he had certainly heard about it, but the others, eager to protect Preveza and ignorant of all but such fire as the ordinary galley could put up, had overruled him.

Their troops now paid the price. As soon as the Turkish janissaries began entrenching themselves along the shore the ships laying off opened up on them, and a massacre ensued. Some of these carracks, as will be seen, mounted as many as twenty-eight guns on each side: bound to stock carriages, they could not be traversed, but only fire straight ahead. Nevertheless, given a fixed target of infantrymen in trenches, and with no shore guns to answer them back, even the janissaries, the bravest of the brave among the famous Ottoman troops, broke and ran, leaving many dead behind them. The great ship armed with its batteries of guns had achieved one of its first recorded successes.

In the naval action which followed, when Andrea Doria and his fleet withdrew from the dangerous coast of Preveza and headed for the open sea, followed close on its heels by Barbarossa's galleys issuing out in pursuit from the narrow channel mouth, the victory lay with the Turks. The genius of Barbarossa, one of the greatest Mediterranean seamen of any time, outwitted Andrea Doria, hampered as he was by attempting to manoeuvre his unwieldy composite fleet. Only one event in the course of the running action need concern us; this featured the *Galleon of Venice* since once again it foreshadowed the course of things to come: the triumph of the heavily built, heavily armed ship.

This vessel, commanded by one of the most able Venetian seamen of the time, Alessandro Condalmeiro, was left behind as Andrea Doria withdrew his fleet towards the south of Levkas island, where he hoped to give battle to Barbarossa. The flagship of the Venetian contingent, she was described as heavily built, heavily gunned, and sheathed with plate below water — all of which made her slow to move in the light wind that was blowing at the time. Finally becalmed off the steep westerly sides of Levkas, she lay dead in the line of advance of Barbarossa's fleet as they rounded the northern tip of the island in pursuit of Andrea Doria's allied fleet to the south.

The Turkish galleys were in fighting order; Barbarossa's flagship in the centre of a great line that curved slightly like a scimitar, with his two ablest lieutenants stationed the one at the head of the starboard wing and the other of the port wing. The moment he had seen them round the cape, Condalmeiro had sent back a rowing boat to his admiral asking for reinforcements, i.e. galleys, to be sent up to lend a hand in the action that must soon begin. It was clear that the enemy could not just ignore his great ship, laid like a challenge in the line of their advance. Barbarossa's solution to the problem she presented was to send in individual squadrons of galleys against her, attacking in one wave at a time, retiring, reloading and then returning. This was the normal practice for galleys when attacking a large stationary object, such as a target on the shore; detached groups often four abreast, 'quadrilles', which marching and countermarching could keep up an almost permanent fire. Assuming that the Turkish vessels were almost identical to the European ones of the time (as indeed they usually were), they would have mounted five guns forward housed on the *rambades,* the strengthened platform at the prow, the principal one being a 'cannon serpentine' firing a 48 or 50 pound ball. On each side of it were two 24 pounders, and outwards of these, but fixed pointing to port and starboard, and only for use in close work where they could be fired broadside, were two short 12 pounders. The three forward guns constituting the main armament could neither be lowered nor depressed, nor traversed from left to right; they were entirely reliant on the direction of the ship's head when firing, and the rise and fall of the sea, as to whether they hit the enemy between wind and water or not. Everything in fact depended upon the judgement and discretion of the gunner as to the exact moment when the pieces were fired.

Conspicuous in full armour on the high aftercastle of his ship, Condalmeiro awaited the galleys' attack. He was dressed as if for a land battle, since at that time, and for some time to come, a sea fight might swiftly turn into a boarding action in which the unarmed sailor of later centuries would have been a liability; in any case, most sea commanders of all nations were still, as they had been in classical centuries, equally army commanders. The tactics of sea warfare (particularly galley warfare) were almost identical with the movements used for troops ashore and, with the exception of a few 'mariners' (specifically trained in sail and rope work, and often fishermen by origin), every man aboard a ship was a soldier first and foremost. As sail predominated over oars and gunnery became more and more important, so a whole new school of tactical thinking and practical training led to the evolution of the fighting sailor. Condalmeiro was of course, like all Venetians of his day, familiar with the sea and he had also mastered the new use of guns afloat. Most of these, and his ship may have had as many as fifty-six excluding light anti-personnel weapons, were probably long serpentines or 24 pounders — giving him a formidable broadside. Being familiar with galley warfare, he will have known that the one thing he must not let them do was to sweep in and strike with the beaked rams, locking ship to ship, while their fighting men swarmed aboard. The high sides of the carrack galleon will have made this more difficult for them than if it had been a galley to galley action, and in any case it is probable that boarding nets had been rigged over the closely spaced spars that normally carried canvas sun awnings.

The first wave of attacking galleys were also the first to open fire, and in this salvo one lucky or well-directed shot brought the mainmast of the Venetian crashing overboard in a tangle of canvas, spars and rigging. Encouraged by the sight of an enemy now immobilized even if the wind did spring up, the galley closed to ram. There had been no return of fire from the galleon, for Condalmeiro's well disciplined crew were waiting until there could be no doubt about their broadsides striking home. As the first wave of galleys came within close range the hitherto silent ship burst into a roar of flame from her deck and dark gunports. In that one moment naval warfare was changed for ever. The days when swift manoeuvrability, the act of ramming, and the storming aboard of boarding parties had been decisive in sea battles were henceforth doomed. The new navy whose ships could accommodate as much armament as a fortress ashore had arrived to determine the fortunes of nations and empires at sea for four centuries — three centuries under sail and one under steam. Condalmeiro's galleon in the only successful part (for the allies) of an action which was itself to be decisively won by the Turks had signalled the end of the two thousand years and more in which the lean man-propelled warship, the galley, had reigned supreme. Devastated by the shock of the broadside the survivors of the first wave withdrew. One galley was sunk on the spot, several others disabled, and the sea around the Venetian ship became agitated by falling masts and screaming men, shattered oars and the cries of galley slaves struggling helplessly at their benches to free themselves.

As this individual action developed, with Barbarossa sending in successive waves of galleys against Condalmeiro's ship, the latter used his guns with careful accuracy, not wasting shot but waiting until a galley stopped or began to turn — firing at the moment when his own gunners had a practically immobile target. His heavily-built vessel could weather the shots from the galleys, which themselves could not withstand a well-directed cannon ball. The conduct of Andrea Doria throughout the campaign and his failure to send any allied galleys to the assistance of Condalmeiro are of no concern here. The subsequent running fight that the battle of Preveza became, rightly hailed by the Turks as a significant victory, signalled in part the long decline of Venice. Barbarossa who had already given the Sultan Suleiman the mastery of the eastern Mediterranean had now given him command of the western basin as well.

Doria's reputation was badly tarnished, but in mitigation of his conduct it must be said that he had no experience of handling a mixed fleet involving sailing ships. Nor had anyone else at the time, and in fact composite fleets of galleys and sailing vessels were shown at Preveza to be something that no one could handle. It is significant that at the famous battle of Lepanto in 1571 — the last sea battle in which both sides fought with oar-propelled vessels — the pure sailing ship was markedly absent. A few years before this, when an allied fleet was going to the relief of Malta, then besieged by the Turks, it was decided on the advice of some who had been present at Preveza not to attempt to act with a composite fleet, but to send galleys alone. The lesson of Preveza had been well learned. But what had not been forgotten by anybody was the action of Condalmeiro's single *Galleon of Venice* when surrounded by galleys. So fierce had been his resistance throughout the day that Barbarossa was compelled to withdraw his attacking squadrons well before sunset. Condalmeiro, despite the loss of his mainmast, managed to sail northward with a favourable wind over night and make his way back to Venice — the only captain and crew of the allied European powers to have distinguished himself in the action.

If it is noteworthy that at Lepanto no sailing vessels were among the fleets, it is also worth remarking that much of the major damage inflicted upon the Turks was due to a type of vessel called a *galeazza*. These galleases, thrown forward of the main battle line by Don John of Austria, broke up the Turks' attack formation and contributed considerably to the ensuing victory. They were indeed 'the great ship' of the time in the Mediterranean, and since some of them were built (with northern modifications) for King Henry VIII's new navy and they even figured in the Spanish armada of 1588, their overall design is important in this history. They were a hybrid between the galley and the galleon, designed to make the best of both worlds and — as is so often the case with such crossbreeds — failing to do either. They were, however, capable of mounting a heavy armament and their effect at Lepanto was largely contributory to Don John's winning the day.

The battle of Lepanto, being important to the Europeans at a time when the Ottoman power seemed everywhere invincible, was naturally recorded by many contemporary artists. The galleases immediately attract attention because of their obvious weight and power. They are three masted — fore, main and mizzen each setting a lateen sail. As in the galleys, the large spars necessary for bearing the weight of the sails are made of two separate pieces fished together in the centre where the spar bears against the mast. Some of them also seem to have a small foremast, akin to a bowsprit, leaning over the great ram. To this is hoisted a square sail, similar to the artemon of classical times and the spritsail of later northern vessels. Pictures of the action at Lepanto as well as a fresco in the Escorial, depicting a battle off the Azores some years later in 1582, show this last of the great ships of an exclusively Mediterranean design, while Anthony Anthony's roll shows it in a slightly altered form to suit northern waters.

While in years to come the hard life of the seamen/ mariner in sailing vessels would engage the attention of many chroniclers and even (as in the case of 'Jack Nastyface' in Nelson's navy) of sailors who wrote their autobiographies, the memory has long since faded of the 'galley slave', although the expression is still used in the language. What that life was like (and it was one into which any traveller by sea might fall in the Mediterranean for centuries) has been described by the Frenchman Jean Marteille de Bergerac:

> The galley slaves are chained six to a bench; these are four foot wide covered with sacking stuffed with wool, over which are laid sheepskins that reach down to the deck. The officer in charge of the galley slaves stays aft with the captain from whom he receives his orders. There are also two under-officers, one amidships and one at the prow. Both of these are armed with whips with which they flog the naked bodies of the slaves. When the captain gives the order to row, the officer gives the signal with a slave whistle which hangs on a cord round his neck; the signal is repeated by the under officers, and very soon all fifty oars strike the water as one. Picture to yourself six men chained to a bench naked as they were born, one foot on the stretcher, the other lifted and placed against the bench in front of him, supporting in their hands a vastly heavy oar and stretching their bodies backwards while their arms are extended to push the loom of the oar clear of the backs of those in front of them.... Sometimes the galley slaves row ten, twelve, even twenty hours at a stretch, without the slightest rest or break. On these

occasions the officer will go round and put pieces of bread soaked in wine into the mouths of the wretched rowers, to prevent them from fainting. Then the captain will call upon the officers to redouble their blows, and if one of the slaves falls exhausted over his oar (which is quite a common occurrence) he is flogged until he appears to be dead and is thrown overboard without ceremony....

Before leaving the genesis of the great warship in the Mediterranean, and passing to its development in northern countries (whose nautical historians often tend to ignore its home of origin) it is interesting to see what size and powerful seagoing character the great ships of the Mediterranean had attained during the sixteenth century. J. Taafe in his *History of the Order of St John* describes the flagship of the Order (referred to by several authors of the period as 'the great carrack of Rhodes'), which was probably the largest warship afloat in its time:

(It) had eight decks or floors, and such space for warehouses and stores that it could keep at sea for six months without once having occasion to touch land for any sort of provisions, not even water; for it had a monstrous supply for all that time of water, the freshest and most limpid; nor did the crew eat biscuit, but excellent white bread, baked every day, the corn being ground by a multitude of handmills, and an oven so capacious that it baked two thousand large loaves at a time. That ship was sheathed with six several sheathings of metal, two of which underwater were lead with bronze screws (which do not consume the lead like iron screws), and with such consummate art was it built that it could never sink, no human power could submerge it. [A rash observation common to all centuries!] Magnificent rooms, an armoury for 500 men; but of the quantity of cannon of every kind, no need to say anything, save that fifty of them were of extraordinary dimensions; but what crowned all is that the enormous vessel was of incomparable swiftness and agility, and that its sails were astonishingly manageable; that it required little toil to reef or veer, and perform all nautical evolutions; not to speak of fighting people, but the mere mariners amounted to 300; as likewise two galleys of fifteen benches each, one galley lying in tow off the stern, and the other drawn aboard; not to mention various boats of divers sizes, also drawn aboard; and truly of such strength her sides, that though she had often been in action, and perforated by many cannon balls, not one of them ever went directly through her, or even passed her deadworks.

Even allowing for some exaggeration, this battleship of the Order of St John (which presumably ended its life in the Order's new home of Malta) was something that was not to be rivalled by any northern country for a long time to come. This undoubtedly was a sailing vessel, pure and simple, its galleys used to tow it through a summer calm or give it a pull in some suitable direction to find a new pluck of wind. Unfortunately we have no record of its dimensions, although this great carrack was presumably the *Santa Maria* in which the Grand Master of the Order and others left Rhodes in 1523 after that island's capture by the Turks. It is reported of this ship that on one occasion in a storm in the Malta Channel she was struck by lightning, nine members of the crew being killed and the Grand Master's sword being reduced to ashes, though he himself was unharmed.

A Venetian manuscript of 1550 gives the dimensions of a large sailing galleon as 135 feet overall, 100 feet on the keel, and 33 feet beam. No doubt the great carrack of Rhodes was even larger, but something like these were probably the dimensions of the *Galleon of Venice* in which Alessandro Condalmeiro successfully fought off the galleys of Barbarossa at the battle of Preveza, thus introducing upon the scene of a famous naval action the type of ship which would rule the future. The rough proportions of 4:3:1 were those which were to obtain in much further shipbuilding. Once the type had been proved seaworthy and workable in windy, tidal seas and the great oceans of the world, it would remain basically unchanged for a long time. This was due not only to the conservatism of naval architects and seamen (though this played its part) but to the limitations of canvas and manpower. Improvements in armaments manufacture would be the main source of change.

CHAPTER TWO

The King and the New Navy

Until the arrival of the gun afloat, naval warfare in northern seas had been carried out in not so different a fashion from the Mediterranean. Since it consisted of little more than raiding from one coast to another, or piratical forays into the Channel, the galley setting a squaresail was as suitable for such short operations as it was in the south. The squaresail as opposed to the lateen on the Mediterranean was a point of difference, as was the fact that the boats were clinker built rather than carvel. It was with such vessels, not unlike those still in use in the fourteenth and fifteenth centuries, that the Vikings had carried out all their great raids and their settlements of England, among other places, while it was also in open, sail and oar-propelled boats that William the Conqueror had launched his successful invasion of England from Normandy. The *drakker* or long ship, manned by oarsmen who were also fighting men, and preceded by flights of arrows as a prelude to boarding (rather than the ram of the south) had been the fighting vessel of the north — carrying the Norse invaders to every available coastline and even as far as the galley-dominated waters beyond Gibraltar. The trade and traffic of the north, however, had been carried in round ships or cogs, usually two-masted, and it was from these, taking some of their inspiration also from the new warships of the Mediterranean, that there was to evolve the true heavily gunned great ship of the future.

Henry VII coming to the throne in 1485 secured for himself, by building or buying, a number of 'king's ships' — the framework on which his son would build a navy. The father however was involved in only one continental war, had no wish for foreign entanglements and, like the practical man of business that he was, used his ships almost entirely for trade and to carry merchandise, even hiring them out to private citizens for these purposes. These were three or four masted, the after, fourth mast being called the bonaventure and invariably setting a lateen sail. Lateens are often set on the mizzen, more rarely on the main, but the foremast invariably sets a squaresail. Battlemented castles formed a part of the bows and stern, foreshadowing the forecastle and the poop of the future. The small guns of that time were very largely defensive, longbowmen and crossbowmen providing the armament if the ship was engaged in close action. Such vessels (allowing for the often unseamanlike eye of silver- and goldsmiths) can be seen in some of the elaborate 'salts' or Nefs made on the continent and in England. (A fine example is the French-made Burghley Nef in London's Victoria and Albert Museum, dated towards the end of the fifteenth century).

Henry VIII took a very different view of kingship to his father. This man of the Renaissance was nevertheless in some respects more backward-looking than his quietly industrious, commercially-minded predecessor. When he came to the throne in 1509 he had basically two options in the field of kingship open to him. The one was to use the fleet which he had inherited to increase his personal income, at the same time concentrating on the financial side of affairs and the maintenance of law throughout his still youthful kingdom. The second option — and the one he chose — was to adopt the European conception of the martial monarch and to establish England as a dominant European power. Whereas his father had clung to the idea that ships of war were an extravagance to be avoided — like war itself — by a prudent monarch, and those that a king needed to retain should be used as far as possible for peaceful trading, Henry VIII looked upon them as a kingly necessity. In his rivalry with Francis I of France, he involved England as earlier kings had done in the intricate maze of politics and the almost interminable warfare of Europe. The resumption of hostilities with France led to the increase in the king's ships being a necessity and not a luxury.

The two principal ships that Henry VIII inherited were the *Regent* and the *Sovereign*, both intended for trade but furnished with fore and after castles and defensively armed with light guns. In his first war with France he followed the medieval pattern, employing carracks and other sailing vessels — merchantmen converted for war and mainly armed with small breech-loading, antipersonnel pieces. Similarly, one of the first vessels built to his orders in 1513 was the *Great Galley* of 700 tons, rowed by 120 oars and carrying some 200 pieces of artillery of varying sizes. (Tonnage was measured by the weight in casks of wine that the hold would carry — a ton in two casks occupying about 60 cubic feet. To arrive at the deadweight displacement, from one-quarter to one-third of the total was then added.) Four hundred to five hundred would have been a large merchantman for the period, so when we learn that one of the first real warships built for Henry VIII was 1000 tons it is possible to understand its importance. The *Henry Grace à Dieu,* or *Great Harry* as she was generally known, was built in 1514, a four-master and probably originally clinker built (at least below water), for she was entirely rebuilt prior to 1540 — as was common practice when the great changeover in construction was taking place to allow for efficient gunports to be cut in the sides.

As originally built she was fitted with 184 guns, most of them of course being light cast brass guns and anti-personnel weapons, but it's noticeable that, on her rebuilding, the number of her guns sharply declined because the size and weight of them had by now been increased. The 'grete yron gonnes of oone sort that come owt of fflaunders' were the forerunners of all those that were to dominate naval warfare through the centuries. As depicted in her new form in 1545 by Anthony Anthony, *Great Harry* has the flat square stern (also accommodating guns) to be seen on contemporary galleons, but the large and somewhat unseaworthy forecastle is similar to the carracks. She is four-masted with topmasts and topgallant masts on the forward three and a topmast on the after bonaventure. The intricacy of such gear and rigging looks like a nightmare to the modern seaman, but then one must endeavour to recall a breed of men who had grown up from boys involved with sailing craft of one kind or another and with a whole world of heavy canvas and rope and (by later standards) inefficient and complicated rig.

A contemporary painting attributed to Vincent Volpe at Hampton Court Palace shows the departure of Henry VIII from Dover in 1520 for his meeting with Francis I of France at the Field of the Cloth of Gold. The picture is in fact a work of the imagination, for the king crossed to France in a squadron of relatively small vessels, but the artist is concerned to depict Henry as the great seafaring monarch, the creator of 'the battleship navy' of England and therefore has shown him with the largest and most imposing vessels of his fleet. It is noticeable that *Great Harry* has a bowsprit setting a spritsail, and equally noticeable are the guns protruding from her ports. Later, after her rebuilding, she carried two complete tiers of guns below her waist.

A predecessor of the *Great Harry* was a ship a great deal more famous now, *Mary Rose*. Named after the King's sister, she was the first battleship to be built in his reign, her keel being laid in 1509. A smaller ship than *Great Harry*, she was reckoned to be 'of the tonnage of 600 tons'. In 1536 she was completely rebuilt and it is as such that she again is shown in the Anthony Roll, the only portrait of her that exists, showing her as she was at the time she sank in action off Portsmouth. As with the *Great Harry* we see a fine example of the new great ship of the time, still carrying the large castles fore and aft, the latter sitting well into the design of the hull but the forecastle protruding in an exaggerated fashion over the bows.

No one with a seaman's eye can look at these early battleships without thinking what hell they must have been to cope with in a strong beam or head wind; the windage (particularly of the forecastle) must have made them almost unmanageable. It is true that they were only designed for comparatively limited operations off the English coast or in the Channel, but one does not have to sail into the great oceans of the world to experience high winds and dangerous seas, and the grey tide-riddled waters of the Channel (with land close on both hands) are as dangerous as anywhere in the world. It is certainly hardly surprising that by the reign of Queen Elizabeth I English ship builders had greatly reduced the size and overhang of the forecastle, so that their ships approximated more to the Spanish and Portuguese galleons that had long been making their voyages into the Atlantic. It is a fact often disregarded by British naval historians, eager to hail Henry VIII's achievements, that by concentrating on the medieval ambition of making England a European power and neglecting the new world that Spain and Portugal were already opening up, Henry made it difficult for his successors to adventure into that area. On the other hand, his continental ambitions caused him to lay the foundations in Portsmouth of a great naval base, to expend money on creating a navy second to none.

An inventory taken of the first *Mary Rose* before her rebuilding shows that in 1514 she carried seven heavy brass guns and thirty-four heavy iron guns, as well as thirty-seven light guns, mostly of iron, giving a total of seventy-eight. A later inventory of 1545, after she was rebuilt, shows that her total was ninety-one, thirty-eight heavy and fifty-three light, but they are distributed throughout the hull both in the sides and stern in logical tiers whereas one may assume that, in her original construction, a limited number of heavy guns were sited in the waist and the majority of light guns in the castles. Like *Great Harry* she is four-masted, with fighting tops below the topmasts, but she does not carry topgallants. Also like the larger ship, both main and foremast yards have sharp hooks on the arms (for cutting like sickles into an enemy's rigging) and a grapnel hangs from the end of her long bowsprit. The upper decks are largely covered with netting against boarders and the banded guns are clearly intended to represent built-up iron guns and the smooth shining ones, cast guns of bronze. During her rebuild she had been uprated from 600 to 700 tons and additional gunners drafted to her. In 1513 when she had been in action against the French her crew had consisted of 120 mariners, 251 soldiers, 20 gunners, 2 pilots, 5 trumpeters and 36 soldiers: such a disproportion between soldiers, mariners and gunners would change during the century as the two latter categories assumed more and more importance.

The guns which distinguished these new great ships and which in their successors were to be the whole purpose of the ship's existence were still reinforced by many longbowmen (as Mary Rose has revealed) as well as men at arms and armoured officers for boarding in the old-fashioned manner. (Mary Rose's normal complement was 415 men, but in her last action off Portsmouth she had, according to the brother of Vice-Admiral Carew who died in her, no less than 700 men aboard.) A great many of these guns, along with so much else, have now been recovered from her wreck and we know a great deal more about their nature and deployment in an early battleship.

The guns of those days rejoiced in a multitude of names that have a sinister poetry of their own. The brass guns, made of a composition of about 100 parts copper to 10 parts of copper and zinc and eight parts tin, included cannons, demi-cannons, culverins, demi-culverins, sakers, and falcons. These were the more expensive, costing about three times as much to manufacture as the iron guns. The latter included port pieces, slings, demi-slings, fowlers, bases, top pieces, hailshot pieces and hand guns. The barrels of the 'built-up' iron guns (the word 'barrel' stems from the fact that the wrought-iron tubes were made in much the same way as a wooden barrel) were originally made of lengths of forged iron placed over a circular core of wood. Red-hot iron bands or rings were then forced over them so that when they cooled they tightly embraced the inner tube. Further iron bands reinforcing the whole were then shrunk on, the inner core of wood was burned out and the 'piece' was complete. At what was to be the breech end a tightly fitting chamber was now fitted and wedged home. Like a modern cartridge case this held the charge and the shot — an iron or stone ball. Each gun had two or more chambers made for it so that, after firing, another one could be swiftly wedged in position. These early iron guns were, then, breech loaders somewhat like modern guns. The big bronze guns were muzzle loaders, cast all in one piece, and thus not presenting the problems that the breech loaders did. The dangers of the early breech loaders, coupled with the fact that they could only with any safety contain a fairly weak charge, meant that the cast bronze guns, loaded from the muzzle and thus presenting no gas escape problems, became the main type of armament in the centuries to come. Despite the awkwardness of the whole process of muzzle loading, cast guns of brass or iron would dominate sea warfare right up to the nineteenth century when the problem of marrying the breech block with the barrel was finally solved. The hailshot anti-personnel weapons such as have been found on *Mary Rose* were also muzzle loaders.

The sequence of events in the use of weapons during this period of the early battleships was as follows: first the cast bronze guns with their longer range opened fire, then the 'built-up' iron guns, then the archers as the ships closed, and finally anti-personnel weapons like the hailshot guns as opposing ships locked together in the old style with grapnels, and the sea fight was transformed into a land battle. We are at a transition stage in the history of the great ship, when the act of boarding still carries the day. No quarter was given in this last phase (except to those marked out by their grand armour as being gentry worth a ransom) and the defeated went overboard, so that they would not be able to retake the ship. The rate of fire will have been slow, the breech loaders of course being faster than the muzzle loaders; the primary aim of this fire of iron and stone shot being to batter the enemy's 'castles' — exactly as in a shore action prior to the act of storming with infantry. The largest guns, the bronze cannons, were set on quite elaborate carriages, the wheels even being of different sizes to conform with the camber of the deck, while the wrought-iron guns were lashed to their carriages with simpler beds and wheels. In the last stages of the run-in towards the enemy the task of clearing his decks was still largely left to the archers — and the English archer was a most formidable member of the ship's company. Hand guns would in due course take its place, but in the meantime the six-foot long bow made of yew with arrows of poplar (tipped with 'bodkin' heads that could pierce armour) and 'bent' by men skilled in the exercise since early youth, remained as deadly as ever. The crossbow favoured in the continent was indeed an efficient weapon but the trouble was its slow rate of fire; while a crossbowman was reloading with a fresh quarrel, the English archer could let loose three or even four arrows.

In her long life, with a battle career that began in 1512, *Mary Rose* had fought in a number of successful actions, distinguishing herself not only in her fighting but also in her sailing capabilities: it is a pity, then, that she should be remembered now for her last action in the battle of Portsmouth in which she sank, not through enemy gunfire but through the inefficiency of her crew and a gust of ill luck. Nevertheless, and taking into full account the wrecking of *Mary Rose,* this is a battle that deserves study since in many ways it exemplifies the current naval practice of the time.

It was 1545 and the French were preparing for an invasion of England on a major scale. Nothing of comparable endeavour had taken place for centuries and nothing equal to it would occur again until 1588 when the Spanish Armada came. Alexander McKee wrote in his *King Henry VIII's Mary Rose* '...it is a mystery why the Spanish Armada is remembered and the French Armada forgotten'. The answer to that lies almost certainly in the fact that, by the reign of Elizabeth, the Renaissance in England was in full flower and the events were recorded by many literate men. The battle of Portsmouth lacked its correspondents, its recorders of genius and its poets: of the few accounts, those of the French cavalry officer Martin du Bellay and John Hooker in his biography of Sir Peter Carew (younger brother of the ill-fated Vice Admiral who went down in *Mary Rose*) are hardly of the calibre of those that survive from that later Armada.

The French invasion of 1545 (which succeeded in a way that the Spanish did not, since it did put many men ashore in battle order) was largely prompted by Henry VIII's action of the previous year when he had increased the English holdings on the mainland of France by adding Boulogne to Calais, two ports opposite Dover which effectively gave him control of the Channel. This was something which, naturally enough, Francis I could not tolerate, and the immediate evidence of Henry's usage of the ports as bases for the capture of French merchantmen in the Channel added to his determination to strike at his old enemy. He was blessed by the fact that Scotland was increasingly hostile to Henry since his capture of Edinburgh, while the Emperor, Charles V who controlled nearly half the continent was, if not hostile to Henry, certainly not prepared to support him in any way. The Emperor was a Catholic, Francis I was a Catholic, and Henry, having broken with Rome, was a known supporter of the Lutherans on the continent.

The French king's plans were straightforward: he intended to land troops in Scotland to support Henry's enemies in the north (this he was unable to do) and also to make a large scale landing in the south east of England to threaten the heart of Henry's kingdom. In his continental engagements Henry, as he neared the end of his life, had sadly depleted the finances of the kingdom. His spending on the navy alone had been prodigious for those times — and now he had the additional expenditure of maintaining captured Boulogne as an English garrison in hostile French territory. The situation before the attempted invasion which led to the battle of Portsmouth was summed up by the Bishop of Winchester at the time: 'We are at war with France and Scotland, we have enmity with the Bishop of Rome, we have no assured friendship with the Emperor....'

The armada which was assembled in the Seine estuary

gives a good picture of this period of transition in naval affairs, bearing in mind always that it was designed for an invasion and not just for a major sea battle. There were 150 'large' sailing vessels; unfortunately no dimensions are available, and how many of these were just merchantships and how many well-armed carracks of the new warship type one does not know. There were also sixty *flouins*, a type of vessel similar to a row barge, described by J. Nicot (1606) as going 'by oar or sail like a galley', but being of higher freeboard than a galley and usually of 40 to 50 tons. Presumably these would transport men and horses alike. In addition there was a contingent from the Mediterranean of twenty-five galleys, crack fighting ships, under Leone Strozzi, admiral of the galleys of Rhodes, and one of the most famous galley commanders of his time. Since it was high midsummer (all being ready by the second week of July) these galleys might well be expected to display to their full advantage their manoeuvrability and the firepower of their forward guns, as well as their speed in a Channel crossing that was, after all, only about a hundred miles. It would not be unlike a Mediterranean campaign: the fact that they would have to meet the firepower of a few new battleships under sail would be obviated by the fact that the attack would not be made unless conditions were right.

Henry, who had a sound grasp of what the command of the sea meant, was not prepared to allow his enemy to assemble at leisure and make his attack at some favourable moment. He sent out Sir Thomas Seymour with a strong squadron to destroy the main body of the French fleet if possible, making use of fireships. (Historians sometimes write as if Drake's use of these in 1588 was some brilliant innovation; they had in fact been used for a long time before him.) Heavy Channel weather, as so often in naval history, prevented Seymour from either drawing the French out to battle or inflicting any damage on them in their secure anchorages, and his own ships suffered severely in the stormy seas. As yet, the new style of fighting ships were unable to keep the sea under all conditions, and the high castles of the carrack-type vessels must have rendered them almost unmanageable. He returned to Scotland with his mission unaccomplished, and seamen and shipwrights set to work to repair the weather damage sustained. By mid-July there were in Portsmouth (or on their way from the West Country) some hundred ships, including *Great Harry* and *Mary Rose,* of which some sixty were warships, manned by 12,000 men, against 235 French warships of varying size manned by 30,000. The number of men in the invasion force may look disproportionate, but it must be remembered that the English had plenty more troops to call on ashore. Henry's new coastal defences were all manned and his main objective, once the French attacked, was to fight a defensive battle off Portsmouth and let the enemy expend his powers, inflicting if possible severe damage on his fleet. The French had just suffered the loss through an accidental fire of their flagship *Carraquon,* reputedly the finest warship afloat, armed with 100 bronze guns, while the next largest carrack available, which had taken her place as flagship, had recently been damaged in a grounding.

On 17 July an advance guard of four French galleys under Baron de la Garde appeared off St Helen's Bay on a still blue day, ideal for galley action. Fourteen English ships, aided by a land breeze, immediately stood out from Portsmouth 'with so great a promptitude and in so fair an array,' wrote Du Bellay, 'that you would have said that they meant to stand resolutely and engage our whole fleet.' The French admiral moved up the rest of his galleys in support and Lord Lisle, in command of the English fleet, came out of harbour to meet the threat. A desultory action at long range ensued, galleys unwilling to come too close to the heavy guns of the English carracks and the latter unwilling to allow the agile galleys to get at them with their bowchasers before retiring. (It was an action such as would be met with in later wars, between the destroyers on the screen of one fleet and heavy ships of the other.) It ended with sundown, the English retiring behind the protection of the guns of Portsmouth on the one flank and the shallows off Gosport, where they were covered by the guns of forts, on the other. The French took up their position for the night in the anchorage off St Helens. (In the Cowdray engraving the actions of more than one day are confused: but *Great Harry* is clearly depicted opening fire at long range against four galleys — as on the first day.)

D'Annibault's plan of action on the following day was to use his galley force to provoke the English and to attempt to lure them out into the open so that his great number could overwhelm them. The calm summer weather that now prevailed was ideal for the galleys — as it was also for Henry VIII's row barges, which were to prove a surprise to the French, who were not expecting any fast 'destroyer-type' ships from the English navy. Henry, in fact, while putting his trust in the great ship, had had a whole class of new light ships built for just such a day as this. We can see what they were like, for more than one of this type is depicted in the Anthony Roll. These 'rambarges' as Du Bellay calls them were distinctive from the galley in being three-masted with squaresails on the fore and main and lateen on the mizzen only. (A galley of Henry VIII's fleet, on the other hand, also depicted by Anthony Anthony, has much the same profile as a French one of the time and also steps only one mast carrying a large lateen sail.) Henry's row barges have sixteen oars aside set in the waist, and are perhaps more like the French *flouins* than anything else. One thing is clear, they are capable of being more useful than the French galleys if there is anything like a wind, but unlikely to be so agile in conditions of calm where everything depends on the rowers. They have quite long aftercastles and more built-up forecastles than a galley, and altogether stand higher out of the water, being designed, it would seem, for tidal conditions around the Solent.

The French admiral, D'Annibault, drew up his fleet in three divisions line abreast, each consisting of thirty-six sail, the galleys forming an advance guard. The latters' orders were to close with the English and provoke them by accurate gunfire from their heavy (about 30-pounders) forward guns, so that they would pursue and come clear of the land and into open water, where the weight of the French Armada would tell. The English plans were, clearly, just the opposite: not to be drawn out but, rather, to lure the enemy closer and closer to the shore, where the hazards of navigation, quite apart from the shore forts, would perhaps take their toll.

In the beginning, fortune favoured the French for, as Du Bellay tells us:

...with the help of the sea which was calm, without wind or force of current, our galleys could be steered and manoeuvred at will to the detriment of the enemy. He, unable to move from lack of wind, lay openly exposed to the destructive force of our guns, which could do more harm to his ships than he could to us; and all the more so, as the English ships were higher and bulkier and easier to hit while our galleys could, by using their oars, manoeuvre so as not to be hit themselves or retreat if necessary.

For about an hour the galleys, trained as we have seen earlier in Mediterranean tactics against forts and stationary targets, executed their formal quadrilles, causing apparently some damage to *Great Harry* although no mention is made of *Mary Rose* or any other of the English great ships being hit. The dead calm and the slack tide allowed a brilliant exposition of the galley's fighting abilities while showing also that the heavy timbers of the great ships could withstand blows that would have devastated the galleys themselves. That none of their own gunfire was successful against the galleys must be laid at the door of their immobility, the great ship's inability (which was to tax it to the end of its days) to effect a heavy broadside without being beam on to the enemy, and the as yet limited means of elevating or depressing the guns efficiently. Then, at last, the ebb tide began to run and with it an offshore land breeze sprang up.

Bosuns' calls sounded down the advance line of the great ships and the sails broke out as Lord Lisle and the assembled ships began to get under way. They had been lying there enduring the French attacks, firing back whenever opportunity offered (so naturally their gun ports were all open) and now they began to gather way, moving with the tide favourable under their keels at ever increasing speed. The galleys, for their part, had been pressing home their attacks with such confidence that it was their turn to be caught in an unfavourable situation. Due to their great length galleys took a long time to turn, and while turning they inevitably exposed their defenceless beam to the enemy. Now, as they began to turn to escape, the remorseless high bows of the great ships bore down towards them. Apart from their light build which meant that even a glancing blow from a heavy ship would overturn or shatter them, their powers of propulsion were more or less gone once their oars were broken. Brilliantly handled, however, as they had been throughout the first part of the action, all the galleys managed to get clear. Once their sterns were presented to the moving mass of the English great ships they could take their time, retreating at a leisurely beat of their oars to lure the enemy after them.

It was during this early phase of the second part of the action (while the great ships were getting way upon them and commencing their chase) that the fatal accident happened to the *Mary Rose*. She sank, as is now well enough known, not through any gunfire of the French but through the incompetence of her crew, coupled with the fact that she was thoroughly overladen with men and with gear. Her gun ports, as in the case of the other great ships, were all open but her lower row of ports, on account of this increased displacement, were dangerously below their intended level. It is also possible (though this can never be known even now) that some or many of her guns were unsecured. Sir Gawen Carew, uncle of the vice-admiral aboard *Mary Rose*, saw that she was in difficulties as she was hoisting sail and slowly turning towards the enemy and the open sea. *Mary Rose* was heeling in a disastrous fashion and Sir Gawen's shipmaster, in answer to his question as to what the other ship was about, answered laconically that if she carried on like that, 'She was like to be cast away'. As he himself surged past the floundering *Mary Rose* in his ship, the 600 ton *Matthew Gonson,* Sir Gawen called across to Sir George Carew asking what was the matter, to which his nephew replied: 'I have the sort of knaves I cannot rule.' It is clear that due to some gross mismanagement in the hoisting of her sails the ship began to heel heavily. As the ambassador of the Emperor Charles V wrote quoting a survivor, 'when she heeled over with the wind the water entered by the lowest row of gunports which had been left open after firing.'

The loss of this great ship did not, however, affect the outcome of the day. The retreating galleys suddenly found themselves menaced. Out from the English fleet there burst the unexpected flotillas of row barges — manned by men familiar with every nuance of channel, tide and coast, and pulling fast in pursuit. The galleys presenting their 'soft' and unarmed sterns were heading in the direction of the French fleet, whither they hoped to lure the English, and now they came under fire from the bowchasers of this new threat.

As Du Bellay wrote:

A few of them followed astern of our galleys at an incredible speed and badly harassed them with their artillery, against which the galleys had no defence, having no artillery astern. Nor could they turn to face their pursuers, for that would allow the enemy fleet to run them down under full sail and capsize them. However, the Prior of Capua, Peter Strozzi, unable to endure this disgrace any longer, and trusting in the agility of his galley, began to wheel round upon the leading English ship which had got ahead of the others and was almost touching with his bows the stern of one of our galleys. But the English ship, being shorter, turned quicker, and steered back towards the English warships.

That ended the chase, while the French, still withdrawing, continued to try to lure the main body of the English fleet out into open water by landing troops upon the Isle of Wight.

D'Annibault had heard that King Henry himself was down on the coast (he was in his newly built castle at Southsea when *Mary Rose* sank) and hoped that the presence of the monarch himself would cause the English to come out and try to stop this invasion of his realm. Lisle, however, was not to be drawn: he and Henry had discussed the whole strategy in detail before the action had begun and the king, profoundly knowledgeable in all matters of war, had given his overriding orders: 'The French were to be lured, if possible, down among the dangerous shoals and currents of the coast and under his new shore guns, but his own ships were not to be tempted to engage the far larger French fleet.' As it turned out, the whole shore action ended in disastrous fashion for the French, and the battle of Portsmouth was over. At sea, the English had suffered the loss of *Mary Rose* and the French the loss of Admiral D'Annibault's flagship — neither through action. The French had also lost a few men aboard the galleys through the English shot and it is possible that the English also had lost a few aboard *Great Harry*, during the period when she came unsupported under the fire of the galleys after the loss of *Mary Rose*.

What is of particular interest in this transition period in the North between the armed carrack and the designed great ship of war is the part played by the galleys and the row barges as protectors forming defensive screens around their battleships. In fact they foreshadow the light cruiser and destroyer screen of future wars. What emerges from this drawn-out action, a battle effectively won by the English since they prevented the French taking Portsmouth or doing any more than some local devastation with loss of life on both sides in the Isle of Wight, was the extreme vulnerability of the great ship.

There can be little doubt that the great ship, which Henry had done more than any other to promote, became an object of suspicion in his eyes. Even while every effort was being made to raise *Mary Rose* from the seabed (where she was in fact to lie until 1982) he was ordering Lord Lisle to form a new squadron of light ships, principally oared. He had witnessed the masterly manoeuvrability of the galleys and the ease with which they could attack his heavy ships under summer conditions (and wars were still fought in summer months), and he was determined to have 'certain of his ships brought to pass to row, to keep company with others of that sort to attend upon the French galleys....' The row barges which had sprung a surprise upon the French galleys at Portsmouth were good enough in their way, but they were not suitable for accompanying the fleet far out into the Narrow Seas. After the battle of Portsmouth it would seem that Henry settled for a two-tier navy. First and foremost still came the heavily gunned sailing vessel, but secondly came a force of oared vessels — galleasses and pinnaces — to accompany the great ships: rather as, in Nelson's day, the line of battle ships had their frigates.

Henry VIII's contribution to the evolution of the great ship is nevertheless outstanding. He was the first ruler of any kingdom to see that the future afloat lay with the heavily gunned sailing vessel. M. Oppenheim in *A History of the Administration of the Royal Navy* has rightly written of him:

> For almost thirty-eight years nearly every year marked some advance in construction or administration, some plan calculated to make the Navy a more efficient instrument. So far as numbers went he made it the most powerful navy in the world, remembering the limited radius within which it was called upon to act. He revolutionized its armament and improved its fighting and sailing qualities, he himself inventing or adapting a type...fit for the narrow seas.... Regulations for the manoeuvring of fleets and the discipline of their crews were due to him. He discarded the one medieval officer of the crown and organized an administration so broadly planned that, in an extended form, it remains in existence today.

All this is true and what is also true is that, even more than his expenditure on warships which led to the English fighting ship becoming preeminent, Henry's main contribution to the navy was in his innovations into administration. The French were also to build very fine ships of this new all-gun type and so were the Spanish and the Portuguese, but both these countries were to lag behind in the organization of their maritime systems. It was this more than anything else that was to give the English the edge over that later and much better known Armada when the time came.

CHAPTER THREE

The Great Conflict

A second *Mary Rose* would fight in the Great Armada of 1588, but by then the appearance of warships would have changed considerably. Indeed, during the intervening years the design and general layout of fighting vessels steadied at a point which, except in terms of detail, size and armament, would alter little for the next three hundred years. Among the many reasons for this was the general exploration of the Atlantic and the other oceans, hitherto almost a special reserve of Portugal and Spain but now to become gradually open to other seamen, particularly those from Britain. What the Portuguese had long ago mastered in their comparatively small, fast, ocean-worthy carvals was to have its effect upon all shipbuilders. The medieval high castles fore and aft, which could not endure high winds and long seas, were to give place to smaller castles aft (for the housing and comfort of the officers) and even smaller and lower ones forward — to become the legendary fo'c'sle of later seamen.

As Björn Landstrom puts it in his classic *The Ship,* talking of the sixteenth century:

Within the period of a hundred years the sailing ship had undergone more profound development than during the 5500 years of its history that had passed and more than was to occur during 400 years to come. The one-masted ship of the beginning of the fifteenth century had step by step, yet swiftly, become two and three masted, had been

given sprit sails and topsails, was fitted with a fourth
mast and later topgallants also. What was to occur after
this was really only polishing and completion.

With the exception of a few shipbuilders, from whom we are
left some drawings in relative detail of the vessels designed
and built by them, we have no records of many of the earlier
ships during this period of transition from the medieval
carrack to the fighting galleon of the Elizabethan age.
Fortunately, for this later period we have several drawings
in a manuscript at the Pepysian Library which clearly show
constructional details and design. These are confirmed by
other contemporary paintings of the Armada period as
well as by a drawing of an Elizabethan man-of-war in the
Bodleian Library. The constructional drawings which may
have been made by a known master shipwright, Matthew
Baker, in 1586 show galleons of the Elizabethan period
which, though clearly related to earlier vessels like *Mary
Rose,* have moved a long way towards the great sailing men
of war that all later centuries would have recognized. The
most significant change is the reduction of the forecastle,
which has clearly ceased to be used as a 'castle' from which
land/sea battles are conducted, while even the after-castle,
though still very much a defensible area, has been greatly
reduced in its height above the water. (There can be little
doubt that the loss of *Mary Rose,* coupled with criticisms
from master mariners and ships' captains, had led the
builders to rethink some of the main elements of ship design.

Ark Raleigh, built in 1587, and supposedly depicted in a
later picture when she had been renamed *Ark Royal* (after
flying Admiral Howard's flag in the Armada campaign),
was such a galleon of the time. Of 800 tons, she was a four-
master, with two gun decks and displaying a new feature,
a gallery which runs forward from the stern on either side
of the half deck. Otherwise she was more like the earlier
great ships in appearance than were the galleons depicted
in the Pepysian Library. An interesting point to notice is the
diminution in the number of her guns: she had a long career,

but at the most she seems to have had forty-four guns and at other times thirty-eight. This was because by now the weight of the guns had increased and an almost standard size — which was to last for centuries — had been evolved as the most efficient ship killer. This was the cast 32- or 30-pounder so-called demi-cannon. All the light-weight guns of the earlier period had been superseded although, of course, the hand gun, as distinct from the long bow or the cross bow, had largely become the man killer for close quarters work.

The privateering (or piratical) exploits of men like Hawkins, Drake and Frobisher in distant seas, usually working against the ships that were the lifeline between the new Spanish empire and their home country, had given them a knowledge not only of deep sea sailing but of the requirements of an able, fast and well-gunned warship — capable of raiding either a convoy or a port and of getting away again with speed. The tendency, as has been seen, was towards the reduction in size of the efficient warship and, while the Spaniards inclined to larger ships that could carry men and merchandise to and from their empire, as well as guns, the British — more intent at that time on commerce raiding — settled for the smaller vessel. As Laird Clowes has pointed out: 'Records of the tonnage of individual ships employed against the Spanish Armada in 1588 show how very small, for the most part, were even the men-of-war of the period; only a quarter were of 600 tons or over, while a full half did not exceed 360 tons.' Commenting on the drawings in the Pepysian Library he goes on to say:

These draughts show that the later Elizabethan ships were well designed, with a good entry and a fine run aft. One drawing, in fact, compares the underwater body of a ship with the form of a fish, and proves that the idea that a vessel should be designed with a 'cod's head and mackeral tail' was by no means confined to the early nineteenth century. The vessels are all galleon-built, with a forecastle set well back from the stem and a long

projecting beak, and they all have the square tuck, or
transom stern of the period.

A fairly typical example of her time was *Revenge* which
achieved fame as the flagship of Sir Francis Drake when he
was second-in-command during the Armada, and went on
to her ever-remembered last fight against the Spanish fleet
in 1591 under Sir Richard Grenville. Built at Deptford in
1577, *Revenge* had the usual colourful decoration of her
upperworks, for medieval practices were still followed in
this respect at least; she was painted green and white.

Ninety-two foot long on the keel she was probably about
130 feet overall, on a beam of thirty-two feet, and stepped
four masts with topmasts. The topmasts could be struck,
and it must be suspected that many of the topmasts shown
in earlier ships in the Anthony Anthony roll were more
often struck than set, their appearance being more with an
eye to pageantry than practicality at sea. She also had, in
common with many others of her time, a bowsprit setting a
sprit sail which was steeved-up to such an degree as almost
to seem like another mast. She mounted a heavy armament,
probably slightly larger than most other ships of her weight
and class, for Drake himself is believed to have increased it;
he was one of the most fervent exponents of the big gun and
the broadside guns on a long continuous gun deck — thirty-
two-pounders. She also had some of the long, five-pounders
known as sakers guns that were on their way out as being
ineffective in broadside work, and probably mostly retained
only as anti-personnel weapons if the fight ever came down
to the old kind of close work. It was of course her guns that
made her so formidable that in her famous last engagement
she was able to fight off for some fifteen hours a succession
of ships some two or three times her size. Much like the
galleys, in such actions ships were sent in waves against a
single ship so that each came fresh and with her guns primed
and loaded, in the expectation that they would find their
adversary temporarily unable to return the fire. Here, as in
much else in later centuries, the British had the advantage

over their opponents of a strict discipline that resulted in efficient gunnery. Such discipline, to be so much deplored by politicians and writers in the age of the common man, was to result in the country's supremacy upon the seas and her acquisition and management of a great empire. Strict indeed it was, but in those harsh times there were no other options.

The main difference between the English ships and the Portuguese and Spanish at the period the Armada has been often enough commented upon — so much so indeed that almost in protest it has sometimes been said that there was little difference between them after all. It was not so much in the weight of firepower that the English had the advantage as in the sailing qualities of their ships which had been built principally for those very seas upon which the Armada was to venture. Thomas Fuller (b. 1608) in his *Worthies of England,* basing his accounts on the gossip of old contemporaries who remembered the events concerned, makes the point admirably when writing about Shakespeare and his circle:

> Many were the wit-combats between him [Shakespeare] and Ben Jonson: which two I behold like a Spanish great galleon and an English man of war. Master Jonson, like the former, was built far higher in learning; solid, but slow in his performances. Shakespeare, with the English man-of-war, lesser in bulk but lighter in sailing, could turn with all tides, tack about and take advantage of all winds, by the quickness of his wit and invention.

The relative shortness of the keel of ships like *Revenge* in proportion to their overall length meant that they were quick and handy in coming about but in any kind of sea must have been prone to pitch. M. Oppenheim in his *Administration of the Royal Navy* makes the significant comment on all the ships and actions of this period:

> It speaks sufficiently for the courage of the Elizabethan sailor that during the whole of the reign only two English

men-of-war were captured by Spain, and then only after desperate fighting against overwhelming superiority of force. [They were the *Jesus of Lübeck* and the *Revenge*]. It speaks equally well for his seamanship afloat and the skill and good workmanship of shipwrights ashore that, with the exception of the small *Lion's Whelp*, no dockyard built ship was lost by stress of weather, by fire, or by running aground. During the same years, and during the same gales, that the English ships weathered successfully, whole Spanish fleets foundered at sea.

Queen Elizabeth herself, although parsimonious in general towards her navy (and nowhere near as knowledgeable as her father, Henry VIII as to its management and administration), nevertheless made sure that the widows of all those who lost their lives in the *Revenge*'s desperate last fight received six months' pension pay. Such consideration was unusual at a time when disabled seamen begged at street corners and widows received nothing. It was significant, as well as indicative of his outlook towards the seamen, that after the Armada campaign Drake played a major part in their welfare. In collaboration with Hawkins he founded the famous 'Chatham Chest', the fund designed to aid poor seamen. This was the first of such welfare trusts ever to be started in England and was the father of innumerable similar organizations that still flourish.

The Armada had been long thought of, conceived not only by Philip II of Spain as a justified punishment upon the English who had constantly harassed his dominions and the lifeline from his empire that nourished his country, but the dream also of all fervent Catholics. The difficulties of mounting such an operation so far from the main Spanish fleet bases and in such dangerous waters as the Channel had never been underestimated. On the occasions when Spanish ships had met English the latter had invariably displayed superior tactics, sailing abilities, gunnery and courage. It was of their tactics that a Spanish agent in England had warned as early as 1574;

> If the fleets come to hostilities, it would be well to give orders, when they [the Spaniards] approach them [the English] that the ordnance flush with the water should be at once discharged broadside on and so damage their hulls and confuse them with the smoke. This is their own way of fighting, and I have many times seen them do it to the French thirty years ago. I advise his Majesty's ships to be beforehand with them and they will send to the bottom all that are opposed to them. This is a most important piece of advice.

It was advice that was not to be neglected, and when the Armada did finally sail some fourteen years after this letter was written, Philip II had seen to it that it carried an immense weight of guns. However, Spanish tactics seem by intent to have remained relatively the same as in previous days, for the ships mounted an amazing number of small light pieces — sakers, serpentines and the like, which under Hawkins' administration of the English navy were already being dispensed with and consigned to the Tower of London armoury, presumably for use by field forces. It would seem from the very fact that the Spanish fleet, out of 2400 guns, mounted some 1300 light weapons that their ultimate aim was still to fight the ship-to-ship style of close combat, followed by boarding. The realities of the new sea warfare which the English had evolved still escaped the Spanish military mind — for it was by a military code and discipline that their fleet was ruled, and their officers were still gentlemen and soldiers first and foremost. The result was that the seamen and also the all- gunners were a lower grade of despised folk — resulting in poor morale among them and that lack of discipline in gunnery which the English had long enforced. Drake's injunction that 'I must have the gentleman to haul and draw with the mariner, and the mariner with the gentleman' would have been completely incomprehensible to those who commanded and officered the Spanish Armada.

Research in comparatively recent years by Professor Michael Lewis and others into the armament and sizes of the Spanish ships has shown that the flagship of Medina Sidonia, the Portuguese *San Martin,* often portrayed in earlier British accounts as if some giant towering over the English men-of-war, was in fact no more than 750 tons by the British method of calculating tonnage, but 1000 by the continental. The largest ships engaged would seem to have been the English *Triumph* and *White Bear* of 1000 tons, although it is true that the composition of the Armada was so numerous that its overall tonnage was far greater, and even in firepower considerably heavier than the English. Many large merchantmen, also of course armed in the fashion of the time, were required to carry about 20,000 troops of the invasion force. Among the armament of this great force there were, it has been calculated, some 160 guns of 50- and 32-pounder calibre, and over 300 24-pounders and a similar number of 18- and 9-pounders. D. G. Browne in *The Floating Bulwark* has made the interesting comment on the heavy armament of the invasion and battle fleet of Philip II:

> For [it] Philip had scoured Europe. In Kipling's 'Hal o' the Draft', Sussex iron-founders are selling guns to Scottish pirates, but when the author wrote 'of the guns that smote King Philip's fleet', perhaps because he was a Sussex man by adoption he did not add that King Philip smote back with cannon fire from the same source. English gun makers had a high reputation, and in Spain their products fetched not only a correspondingly high price per ton, but even pensions for manufacturers so unpatriotic as to smuggle them over. The Armada had many English guns.

Then as now the armaments industry was international, concerned with money and not scruples. It will be remembered that many of the finest guns in Henry VIII's fleet were of continental origin. It was during Henry's reign that the first gun foundries were started in England and had set in motion the country's whole armaments industry so as to be independent of continental sources.

On 12 July 1588, after all the many delays and misadventures which had befallen it since the beginning, 'The most happy Armada', now renamed 'the Invincible', finally sailed from Corunna under the overall command of the Duke of Medina Sidonia. All in all, considering the times, the difficulty of communications, of land transport and of the whole organizational science relating to *matériel*, it was an astonishing triumph. It would be centuries before anything comparable would be attempted, and it is right to say that only the great empire of Spain at that moment and under Philip II could ever have achieved it. A small country like England with its limited population, its ignorance of the management of empires and of large-scale organizational requirements, could only be fearfully astonished. In common with what has subsequently become their general strategy for the navy over the centuries — to use whichever of several large harbours are closest to the enemy of the moment — they had made Plymouth their main base for this threat from the Atlantic approaches. Here Lord Howard of Effingham flew his flag in *Ark* (later *Ark Royal*) a new warship of 800 tons, with Drake his vice admiral in *Revenge* and Hawkins in *Victory* also of 800 tons. The queen, having heard of early misfortunes to the Spanish fleet, had suggested that some of these large galleons might now be paid off for she was always conscious of the drain on the royal purse when so many of the ships for which the Crown itself was responsible had to be manned and maintained. Howard, however, had insisted on keeping them in commission, displaying in this disagreement with his sovereign the same imperturbable common sense as he did also in his dealings with the fiery and less disciplined Drake. As Sir Julian Corbett remarked of him,

> ... While the crisis lasted he bowed with fine humility to the subordinate, whom he recognized as the greater genius; and yet in giving way he never lost dignity or forgot for a moment that it was he who was responsible for the tone of the fleet. From first to last he set an example of untiring labour, of loyal devotion, and of buoyant courage that is hardly to be surpassed and which entirely won the respect of his headstrong and self-confident Vice Admiral.

While the English waited the Spanish fleet came on steadily with a fine and favourable south wind for their passage towards the Channel — the same wind that held the English in their ports turning into a south-westerly as it rounded the shoulder of the Continent. Lightships were out, however, permanently on watch into the Atlantic, fulfilling then, as later, the scouting capacities for which they were built. This same wind, which had earlier (at gale force) caused the English to turn back from their attempt to catch the Armada in its home ports, was later hailed by Admiral Howard as a blessing in disguise: 'The southerly wind that brought us back from the coast of Spain, brought them out,' he wrote. 'God blessed us with turning us back.'

It was on 19 July that Captain Thomas Fleming in his small barque the *Golden Hind* (called appropriately enough after Drake's famous ship with which he had circumnavigated the world) sighted the first sails. He was on patrol off the Scilly Islands when he saw what was no more than the advance guard of the Armada, lying with sails struck for the others to catch up and rejoin. Hastening back to Plymouth, Fleming brought the great news for which all had been waiting. On the face of it the Spaniards had a tactical advantage, having the weather gauge of their enemy with the bulk of his ships penned in harbour to leeward. Such would indeed have been the case if the Channel had been the Mediterranean at a similar time of year, tideless and with winds from a more or less constant direction — if any wind at all. But it was not, and the English ships were built for their unpredictable climate and their captains were familiar with every ebb and flow of their tides and their errant currents. Neither Philip II nor his admiral were aware that nearly the whole of the English fleet had been committed to the Channel mouth and Plymouth, and their grand strategy was based on a false premise: that the English would come out from the variety of ports available to them down the length of their Channel coastline and would be fought piecemeal during the passage.

Medina Sidonia's orders were to make his way up Channel, not attempting any English port *en route,* and after reaching the North Foreland off Margate establish a beachhead at the mouth of the Thames. The assumption was that he would meet and defeat some of the English ships at the mouth of the Channel, others further up, and finally encounter Admiral Howard with the bulk of his ships in the narrow seas near Dover. Equally false, of course, was the assumption that the Duke of Parma's troops would be able to cross from the Netherlands, where the entire coast was controlled by the handy, shallow-draught vessels of the Dutch.

That first night, the bulk of Howard's ships had warped out of Plymouth Sound and anchored in the lee of Rame Head, which shelters Plymouth from the west. Next morning the south-westerly freshened up again and the English at once began to beat out to sea on the starboard tack. By noon fifty-four of Howard's ships, some great but most small, were standing out to sea to leeward of the Eddystone. Ten further ships, which had missed the first tide, were to join them later. At the same time in Medina Sidonia's flagship, *San Martin,* a last council of war was held before the great Armada commenced its progess up Channel.

CHAPTER FOUR

Tactics and the Armada Campaign

The main subject which came up for discussion was how far up Channel to go before ascertaining what were the exact arrangements with the Duke of Parma? Their unequivocal decision was not to proceed to the North Foreland, as His Majesty had instructed, for the sensible reason that beyond the Narrows there was no good deepwater port. Caught by anything like a northerly or an easterly they would undoubtedly be lost. Beyond the Isle of Wight they would not go until a definite rendezvous with Parma had been arranged. This decision was immediately conveyed back to Philip II by one of the numerous sharp, fast sailing boats that attended upon the great fleet. Medina Sidonia was a stickler for the command regulations of his day.

Another point during the discussion arose from a suggestion that, before proceeding any further, they should fall with all the weight of their ships and men upon this port that lay under their bows — Plymouth. Medina Sidonia politely informed them that such would be quite contrary to the orders of His Majesty, and that furthermore he had good information that the approaches were strait and dangerous, and menaced by shore guns. (Had they tried it, the saga of the Armada might have been relatively short.) They would proceed, then, up-Channel — not beyond the Isle of Wight — until they had further clear news of Parma's intentions.

The English tactics, naturally, were to get out from the coast and the unfavourable position of a lee shore, to windward of this great fleet. Signalling was in its infancy in those days, but no signal was necessary for this declared and simple intention. They had the advantage of sailing in home waters. What's more, even if unwittingly (as most of their good fortune was to happen to them over the centuries), the English had discovered the secret of naval warfare: the broadside, delivered as accurately and as fast as possible. The Armada campaign was to confirm them in the tactical use of weaponry, although the discipline of the battle fleet in line ahead was something that still lay in the future. In view of the known preponderance of soldiers aboard the Spanish and Portuguese vessels the old style type of action was clearly not to be considered — boarding was out. The object, just as now, while the English ships beat out to eastward of the Armada, was to gain the weather gauge; and having done so to attack the enemy's weathermost ships. Unsupported by their fellows to leeward, these could be engaged one after the other by divisions of the English ships, acting as almost independent units following their leaders. Each would then come about in succession, passing their opponents on the opposite tack, as they cleared the last ship of their own lines. Things had come a long way since the battle of Portsmouth, even though the basic principles of the broadside had been understood in 1545. What made the current tactics feasible at all was that the English ship design had come a long way — and in this the disaster of *Mary Rose* may well have played its part.

If the English tactics were only carried out in a ragged and confused manner, they were still sufficiently alarming to the great enemy fleet, which had encountered nothing like them before. But if this was the case, so was the dismay of the English at seeing how their adversary advanced. The Armada displayed exactly that disciplined and composed manner of approach that had been the standard adopted by all Mediterranean fleets for centuries. Galley tactics had been carefully worked out, going back to the time of Salamis and other battles before it. The precision of the Armada's movements and its discipline, which amazed the English at the time and continued to be remarked upon with surprise by naval historians of the north, were common to all fleet encounters in that sea which had given birth to the history of navigation. The Duke of Medina Sidonia was bringing up Channel the largest fleet, certainly in tonnage, that the world had ever seen. It was manoeuvred much the same as a well-disciplined army ashore (the basis of galley tactics) with an almost scientific precision — an excellent performance in the light of its long voyage amid not always happy weather conditions. The English who saw it tended to describe it as like a crescent or a half moon. Of course ships, however well disciplined, could not maintain a curved section, but this no doubt was its appearance; the *lines,* of course, of its four main divisions being kept as such. Although far greater in size and components, it was almost exactly the formation that had been used by Barbarossa in his triumph over the Christians at Preveza in 1538. This according to Filippo Pugafetta (Rome 1588) was the 'eagle' formation, the vanguard forming the head, the advance screen of pinnaces when called back on sighting the enemy the neck, the main battle line the body, the fleet supports the tail, and the two flank divisions forming the wings.

From flank to flank it embraced a wide front of some four miles, making it difficult to outmanoeuvre to get at the rear, while the vanguard of powerful forces was designed to break up any enemy formation early in the action. By having the tips of these wings hardened by some of his best fighting ships Medina Sidonia had ensured that if the English got the weather gauge of him on either flank they would find nothing soft to bite upon. On the other hand, if the enemy were to work around the wings to get at the storeships and transports in the rear they would soon find out that the tips of the wings had dropped back and cut them off. If, on the other hand, they were to elude the strong head in an attempt to slide past and break through the centre, the wings could enfold them and they would be swallowed. The maintenance of this classic formation, even allowing for the fact that they had a favourable west-south-westerly behind them, amazed the independent-minded (and often disobedient) English. To keep the formation the sailing ships furled topsails or spread more canvas with what seemed uncanny precision, while the great galleasses on the wings increased or decreased the oar-beat, maintaining accurate station.

As the sun set on 20 July the wind brought up some rain, and the English, having taken their first awed sight of the weight and number of the Armada ships, drew out further southward into the Channel on the starboard tack. The others who had come out late from Plymouth tacked along the coast between the Armada's northern wing and the shore. Howard and Drake and the main body meanwhile came about on to the port tack during the small hours and stood northerly again towards the coast. If they had all been somewhat astounded by the size of the invading fleet (not partially broken up by storms as they had heard) it was the turn of the Spaniards on the morning of the 21st — when they saw that the bulk of the English fleet was to weather of them. Medina Sidonia and his vice admiral Juan Martinez de Recalde now realized that their information that the main body of the enemy fleet was much further up the coast, with only a small number in Plymouth, was totally incorrect. It was difficult for them to understand how so many ships had got round to weather of them unobserved during the night. Howard himself did not find anything strange in this achievement, commenting in his laconic fashion: 'The next morning being Sunday, all the English that were come out of Plymouth recovered the wind of the Spaniards two leagues to the Westward of the Eddy stone.'

The Spaniards were later to remark that the English ships were 'built very low at the head', and this was one of the design qualities of the new ships that gave them such an advantage in windward work. They had done in two tacks what would have taken the more old-fashioned, high-pooped and high-forecastled galleons of the Spaniards four or maybe more. The finer underwater hulls of the type of design which have been mentioned had also helped them and, for credit must surely be given him, some mention must be made of Hawkins and others for a building programme that had looked ahead instead of staying conservatively in the past. The Spaniards and Portuguese and others with them had the backbone of Mediterranean shipbuilding behind them, further adapted for ocean passages between Spain and America. This meant that windward work was something that they did not have to live with, as did English seamen, for the outward passages were by the southern trade route and the return passages with the Atlantic westerlies behind them. High castles forward and aft meant little under those conditions and, since they accommodated more military, both fore and aft, the castles still served their old purpose.

The main action of the day began with the English under Howard discharging a broadside as they passed the outer wing of the Armada and then, rather than making any further attempt on the main body of the fleet, cramming on all sail and heading for the coast. Howard rightly suspected that the enemy might have intentions upon Plymouth, which he had uncovered by getting to windward of the enemy. The aim now was to attack the enemy nearest the coast and drive them on beyond Plymouth Sound.

Howard in *Ark* and those with him accordingly poured their broadsides into the rearmost ship, *Rata Coronada,* of Don Alonzo de Leiva, while the great carrack, *Regazona,* fell back to render assistance. Neither side would seem to have suffered much damage in this encounter and Howard wrote: 'We made some of them to bear room to stop their leaks. Notwithstanding we durst not adventure to put in amongst them, their fleet being so strong...' Now Drake in *Revenge,* Hawkins in *Victory* and Frobisher in *Triumph* engaged Vice-Admiral Recalde in his galleon *San Juan* on the seaward wing of the Armada. Recalde, most experienced of all the commanders of his fleet, did not attempt to sail placidly onward as the enemy attacked but swung his great galleon round so as to be able to give these passing English broadside for broadside. His action was also calculated to make his enemy attempt to complete the battle in the only way he still reckoned such issues were dealt with — by boarding. But the English had their orders and they knew by now that battles at sea were won by ships fighting ships, and not by boarding parties and the weight of armed men.

After an hour in which *San Juan* had well withstood the long range tactics of the English, others of the seaward wing dropped back to aid and reinforce Recalde. The general mêlée which Recalde had hoped to provoke, with ship against ship actions ending in boarding, was not accepted and Drake and those with him moved out of range and made sail to work round behind the Armada and join Admiral Howard who was now on the inshore wing. They could not know that the decision had already been taken at the Armada Council of War that no attempt would be made on Plymouth and felt gratified that the fleet continued on up Channel, congratulating themselves on what seemed to be the success of their harrying tactics. Despite further attempts by turning some of his ships back on the English to bring about a general action at close quarters, Medina Sidonia found that they refused to be drawn and as the official log records: 'The enemy having opened the range... he could do nothing more, for they still kept the weather gauge, and their ships are so fast and so nimble they can do anything they like with them.' The Armada had in fact suffered relatively little damage and continued on its way with its discipline unimpaired. The English for their part were disappointed that their shot had taken so little toll and if they had expected any collapse of its formation or signs of panic had found none. Drake wrote: 'The 21st we had them in chase; and so coming up to them there hath passed some common shot between some of our fleet and theirs; and as far as we perceive they are determined to sell their lives with blows...'

It was not until after the action was well over that a disaster occurred in the great fleet: this was an explosion aboard the galleon *San Salvador* which blew away a large section of her poop. This was almost certainly due to an accident, for such were not so uncommon in the comparatively early days of wooden warships when stringent regulations on fire control had hardly been sufficiently formulated. The badly damaged ship was later taken in tow and brought into the centre of the Armada, while the whole fleet almost came to an organized standstill during the rescue operation, before proceeding as before. Other things, however, had gone wrong with the Armada; two ships had collided and one of them, *Señora del Rosario* had lost her foremast. She fell behind during the night and was later picked up by Drake. The flagship of Pedro de Valdez, General of the Indian Guard, who apparently made no effort to fight off his enemy, she was a fine 46 gun ship and would have been a match for any vessel in the English service. Her surrender was not conducive to good morale in the Armada, nor was the subsequent loss of *San Salvador* which had leaked so badly after the explosion that she had to be abandoned. Her crew failed to scuttle her or blow her up and she, also, was captured and later towed into Weymouth. English morale afloat was definitely raised by these two accidents and, when the news reached the coastal dwellers and was quickly passed on ashore, it was seen as proof of the navy's superior prowess. In fact, the capture of both these vessels would seem to have been due to poor seamanship on the Spanish part. *Rosario* should never have been surrendered (and in any case had had a good many hours in which to fix a jury rig in place of her lost foremast), while *San Salvador* should never have been abandoned, but scuttled.

Howard's main concern of course always was to prevent the enemy from making a landing at any of the available places *en route*; he could not know that Admiral Medina Sidonia had already determined at the Council not to proceed beyond the Isle of Wight. The wind fell completely away on the late afternoon of the 22nd, and all ships were becalmed, the oared vessels in the Armada having perforce to stay with the sailing vessels. In view of the Armada keeping its formation no separate action could be initiated by vessels that were capable of it, and the awkwardness of handling composite fleets was revealed once again. Next morning an easterly came up with the dawn, giving the Spaniards the weather gauge — but it was something that they could not take advantage of (as they would have done if this had been a straight fleet action), being constrained by the nature of their objective to press on. Howard, worried that the enemy would try to weather Portland Bill and land in Weymouth tried to drive the inshore wing of the Armada away from the land. He had little success for, determined not to be outflanked, Medina Sidonia brought back his galleons on that wing to intercept the English line. A running battle occurred when Howard's ships, having tacked inshore, sailed back in a south-westerly direction to try and get to weather of the Armada's seaward wing. He was frustrated again by the Spanish rearguard immediately dropping back. In Camden's account, 'the great guns rattled like so many peals of thunder', but little if any damage was done on either side. What did occur of course was a great expenditure of powder and shot, something that throughout the campaign the English could only repair with great difficulty by detaching much needed ships into ports, and which the Armada could not repair at all.

During this action on the seaward wing the heavy ships of the Armada would constantly fall back to prevent the English from getting round, at the same time trying to provoke them to boarding actions. The new naval warfare was pitted against the old. Meanwhile, on the inshore wing of the great fleet, another struggle was developing, where Frobisher in the 1000-ton *Triumph* in company with five other smaller ships, and separated from the main body of the English fleet, had been cut off inshore. The strong Spanish wing — four galleasses 'assaulted them sharply' — had the advantage that, as the day wore on, the wind veered into the south, thus putting them to windward of Frobisher. Howard, disengaging from his action on the seaward wing of the Armada, and taking advantage himself of this wind shift made to come down with sixteen other ships to help *Triumph*. During his engagement Vice-Admiral Recalde's flagship *San Juan* had been severely damaged and forced to withdraw and now, as Howard headed down the rear of the Armada the admiral himself, Medina Sidonia, in his flagship the great *San Martin* fell back to meet his English counterpart in *Ark Royal*.

In a gesture that belonged to an age that was past Medina Sidonia struck his topsails — the invitation to the other to come aboard and 'fight like gentlemen'. This Spanish courtesy was disregarded by the rough Lord Howard and the others with him. They raked *San Martin* with their broadsides as they passed but refused to close within grappling range. The English line passed, tacked and repassed, and for a full hour Medina Sidonia's flagship endured their fire — suffering heavily herself, but continuing to fight on with a courage quite equal to her opponents. In due course, seeing their admiral so beset by the English, other galleons dropped back to aid her. Refusing to become mixed up in a mêlée which might have led to boarding actions, Howard and his ships passed on to assist Frobisher. But the latter was no longer in need, the galleasses had withdrawn, and the wind had now gone round to the west, thus putting the English to the weather of the Armada.

The battle of Portland Bill, as it came to be called, taught both sides a lesson. The Spanish learned that the old style naval warfare was over, against ships that were both manoeuvrable and heavily gunned. The English learned that heavily-built wooden ships were almost unsinkable unless a steady rate of fire could be poured into them by ships passing in a regular and disciplined line. Of course the implications were not fully grasped at the time, but looking back on this and other later actions men grasped the idea of the necessity of the line of battle: heavy ships, with a great weight of metal, moving with precision like one giant warship a mile or more long to overwhelm their opponents. The English had sensed the necessity of this line but they had not the discipline nor the signalling capability to achieve it. Their ragged attacks had badly damaged some of their opponents, but they were still afloat.

The main problem for both sides at the moment was ammunition. The English had left Plymouth with about thirty rounds per gun and powder for the same, and were now practically without ammunition. Although fast ships were despatched to all coastal ports to bring back fresh supplies these were hard to come by, and for the rest of the campaign ships were forced to conserve their shot. The Spanish for their part had embarked on the expedition with about fifty rounds per gun, which had been considered more than enough, and had run into the kind of action that they had not expected — where powder and shot were all. Off a hostile coast, they had no chance of further supplies unless they got them from the Duke of Parma — and still they heard nothing from the duke, imprisoned as his own ships were by the hostile Dutch. Although no one could know it at the time, the Invincible Armada was already doomed — even if the weather in the end had not taken its hostile course. But its discipline did not falter and, while the English sent ashore for more ammunition and continued to follow in its wake, the great Armada continued on inexorably up Channel.

At dawn on 25 July the two fleets were again becalmed — only some forty miles east of the scene of their last engagement — off the Isle of Wight. Howard's concern again was naturally that the enemy would attempt a landing on the island — and they had much more chance of success than the French in 1545, for they had the arms and men to secure a permanent foothold. On this day a confused fight took place on the Spanish seaward wing where a galleon, *Gran Grifon,* had fallen back out of the close order and was immediately pounced on by Drake in *Revenge.* Soon the whole Spanish right wing was engaged, but *Gran Grifon,* although taking heavy punishment, was taken out of danger by galleasses sent by Medina Sidonia. In the course of this day's battle the English must have realized one sad fact — they were unlikely with their tactics and available shot to sink any of the Spaniards — while the latter realized that there would be no close action accepted by the English where their own weight of soldiery might have told. As matters stood it was something like a stalemate, which might only be altered by some change in the weather.

Ideal invasion weather it certainly was, but hearing nothing from Parma the Duke of Medina Sidonia dare not effect a landing anywhere. Later off the Isle of Wight a wind sprang up from the south west enabling Drake to press home an attack on the seaward flank of the Armada while Frobisher and the ships with him, being inshore, had some difficulty in slipping clear away to the rear of the left wing. The attack to seaward on the other hand was going well, the post of honour there, in place of Recalde's damaged flagship, now being held by *San Mateo,* a large Portuguese galleon. Forced to retire by the harassing tactics and fire of the English, her place was taken by the great galleon of the Duke of Tuscany, *Florencia.* But gradually, as the English, having the weather gauge as well as the advantage of their manoeuvrability, tacked back and forth to seaward this whole section of the Armada formation began to yield, forcing ship after ship as they endeavoured to keep station to edge towards the English coast. It is possible, and indeed probable in view of his immense knowledge of the Channel, that Drake and his ships were deliberately trying to drive the Armada on to one of the major hazards of this dangerous coast.

Ten miles east of the Isle of Wight lie the Owers — that formidable bank of shoal water, toothed in places with rocks. In the days of sail it claimed many victims, and indeed in 1545 it had been one of Lord Lisle's hopes that he could inveigle the main French fleet close inshore onto the dangers of this area. Medina Sidonia observed the way his fleet was being edged to the north east at almost the same moment as his principal pilot reported shoaling water to port of the fleet. An immediate signal was made by gunfire and the Armada, following their admiral, altered course and started to draw offshore in a south-easterly direction. The Isle of Wight began to fade behind them and the English ships also drew off — once again they were almost out of powder and shot. Howard probably rightly considered the day a victory, for the feared landing on the Isle of Wight had not taken place, and the enemy were now standing away from the English coastline.

Hawkins wrote of the day's action: 'It was a hot fray, wherein some store of powder was spent, and after all, little done.' The Duke of Medina Sidonia for his part sent an immediate despatch to the Duke of Parma begging him for ammunition and asking him to provide forty small ships to join the Armada. He had determined to head across Channel for Calais, where he hoped to be able to reammunition as well as find out what preparations were made for the transit of the main body of troops. Clearly, there could be no invasion unless his fleet was able to fight off the English navy, and until he had an adequate supply of invasion barges together with Parma's troops to man them. His own military force carried in the Armada was designed to make a landing, hold a beachhead, and even open the way to London, but without the necessary backup of arms and men they could do no more. The more than unfortunate Medina Sidonia, who was to end his days in the misery of obloquy, had been given a task that was quite beyond the economic or military planning capability of the age, and the man who had given it to him was quite ignorant of the realities involved in an expedition like the Armada. King Philip II in his strange eyrie of the Escorial, from which he conducted all the affairs of his giant empire, had no real knowledge of sea affairs and had planned everything as if it was no more than a major military expedition. He could not have envisaged the circumstances of the time when, as his admiral put it: 'the heaviness of our ships, compared with the lightness of theirs, rendered it impossible in any manner to bring them to close action...'

On the afternoon of 27 July 1588 the great Armada came to anchor in the roads off Calais. The English ships, which had been snapping at its heels like terriers all down the Channel, had never been able to break that formidable order and now, as they crossed in its wake towards France, they almost certainly assumed that the enemy were doing no more than swing across Channel before coming back on the other tack to head for Dover, the Downs, or the North Foreland. When the Spaniards came to anchor with their usual immaculate precision the surprised English saw nothing else but to follow their example. And so both fleets lay with a mile or less of water between them off Calais. Lord Henry Seymour, Howard's cousin, who had been guarding the Downs, now crossed the Narrow Seas to join the rest of the fleet. While the Duke of Medina Sidonia sent further messages to Parma, Howard and his captains met in Council.

As the English saw it, and as the Spaniards were to anticipate, there was only one solution to an enemy fleet that had apparently taken refuge and that was to smoke them out, with fireships. In the days of wooden ships, where fire was always the greatest hazard (and especially since the arrival of gunpowder on board), the use of fire against an enemy was a well tried weapon. The sophisticated Byzantines had long ago perfected their Greek fire, pumping an inflammable liquid through hollow tubes set in the bows of their warships. The simpler Elizabethans loaded their fireships with any available combustibles, shotting and priming their guns so that they would go off when the heat in the vessels grew intense, and releasing them down upon their enemy. They were to weather of the Armada, but they waited until the floodtide was making into Calais. Then, with wind and tide behind them, the fireships were released on that great and hitherto so disciplined fleet.

The main reason for what subsequently seems the excessive alarm displayed by the ships of the Armada (which had thrown out a screen of small ships to protect and tow away any fireships) was the event of Antwerp three years before. The Italian engineer Giambelli (at that moment, it was known, working for Queen Elizabeth) had devised for the Dutch a fireship that was more like an enormous bomb, lined with bricks and loaded with gunpowder, on top of and around which stones and scrap iron were packed. When that had been released by the Dutch and had gone off among the Spaniards it had caused more devastation than had ever been known since the invention of gunpowder, and had left more men dead than the amount of casualties to be expected on a large battlefield. Small wonder that Medina Sidonia and his other officers were afraid that 'the devil' Drake was sending against them something similar.

In the event, the fireships were no more than expendable vessels hastily got together; the effect on the Armada, however, was as if a host of deadly Antwerp 'hellburners' had been unleashed. While some of the ships followed their admiral's orders of methodically slipping their cable after buoying it and then standing out to sea, others merely let it run without buoying, or hacked through their cables and moved off. Medina Sidonia, himself, made a short tack out to sea clear of the advancing fireships and then reanchored. Had the rest of his fleet followed his example they would have come to no harm, for the ships merely swept on with the tide, mostly to burn quietly on shore. Not a single Spanish ship, as far as can be learned, was sunk by the fireships; but their effect on morale was disastrous. Nothing that the English had achieved during the passage of the Channel had managed to break the magnificent discipline and order of the Armada; but the fireships did.

As I wrote in *Drake*

From this moment on the Armada was a dying animal. It had entered the Channel like a bull coming into the arena — self-confident, tossing its horns, and eyeing the matador with disdain. It had been harassed, picadors had lanced its shoulders, and banderilleros had planted their darts in its humped muscles. Now the bull had found its *querencia* — a corner of the ring where it felt secure — only to be driven out of it by 'firecrackers'.

The ragged, running battle that followed off Gravelines and the final tragic fate of the Armada need not concern us here. As far as the English were concerned, though they were not to be certain of this for a number of days to come, the campaign was over.

There are many accounts of the Armada, some stressing this and some that — depending largely on the period in which they were compiled and the points which the authors wished to emphasize. One thing remains consistently true: the new tactics for sea battles had been learned, even though in 1588 it was too early to apply them. Broadsides of heavy metal, delivered by ships acting in disciplined fashion in line ahead, were to be the secret of success in the future. This implied the triumph of the ship of the line, the great ship, having excellent sea-keeping ability and endurance, coupled with manoeuvrability and firepower.

CHAPTER FIVE

The Seventeenth Century

Looking back over the early centuries when shipbuilding in northern Europe was acquiring such importance, it is surprising how little we know with any exactness of their basic dimensions and construction. But then, to look even further back in time, the subject of the dimensions and construction of the great ships of antiquity can still arouse argument among scholars, and it would be easier to reconstruct the Parthenon or the Colosseum as they were than any of the ships that served their cities and their cultures.

For instance, the measurements, tonnage and rigging of so famous a ship as Sir Francis Drake's *Pelican* — later renamed the *Golden Hind*, in which he circumnavigated the globe — are unknown. Of course, she was no great ship: that we do know, for a bond given by 'Francis Drake of Plymouth', before the voyage or his knighthood, has her as 150 tons. Too small, one might have thought, to cause such a panic on the Pacific coast of Spain's New World, let alone carry back a fortune. Yet this was indeed the ship in which Drake was knighted by his queen, and which was so famous as to be mentioned by Ben Jonson in one of his plays, and to be commented upon by Holinshed in *Chronicles*. Jonson suggests that she should 'be fixed upon the stump of Paul's steeple, in lieu of the spire, that, being discerned far and near, it might be noted and pointed at of people with these true terms: "Yonder is the bark that hath sailed round the world."' The fact is that shipbuilders and people in general of that time had little concern, let alone sentimentality, about the past. Drake's ship, however, was considered important enough for her to be preserved for nearly a hundred years in a dry dock at Deptford. Only from the known measurements of the brickwork of this dock (Laird Clowes) can her most probable dimensions be calculated: keel, 47 feet; stem to stern-post, 60 feet; breadth 19 feet; hold depth 9-10 feet; tonnage about 100. It was not until later in the seventeenth century that shipbuilding became more regularized, annotated by body plans, and attempts made towards some systemization. Until then, the sardonic comment of Captain George Weymouth, a professional in an age of skilled but unlettered craftsmen, must surely have often been true, that he 'yet could never see two ships builded of the like proportion by the best and most skilful of shipwrights though they have many times undertaken the same...because they trust rather to their judgement than their art, and to their eye than their scale and compass'. Oppenheim remarks: 'As a practical illustration of the shipwrights' loose methods of calculation it may be mentioned that when the *Prince Royal,* the largest vessel of the reign [James I], was built, Phineas Pett and Bright estimated that 775 loads of timber would be required, whereas 1627 loads were actually used, and the general increase in her cost by this error of judgement was £5908.' Of course, long after the dawn of the scientific age, errors of calculation have often been made (especially when it comes to matters of costing!)

Just as *Great Harry* and (more recently) *Mary Rose* are quoted as examples of the great ships in the reign of Henry VIII, so *Prince Royal* or *Royal Prince* (1610) and *Sovereign of the Seas* (1637) seem to epitomize the era that followed the Elizabethan. A principal reason for this, of course, is the fact that we have pictures of both of them — Payne's engraving of the latter being probably one of the best known early ship pictures in existence. Both these great ships still showed a close affinity with those of the Elizabethan period in such details as the square tuck stern and the same galleon bow with its low, long beakhead.

The *Prince Royal* carried 56 guns on three complete gundecks, ending her life after two further rebuildings, with 90 guns. In proportions she differed little from her predecessors, although she was about 200 tons larger and was decorated with an extravagance of gilt and carving that would certainly not have been found on any of the Armada ships. Built in 1610 by Phineas Pett, one of the foremost shipbuilders to be historically recorded and a man of good education and technical knowledge, she had length from stem to stern post of slightly less than four times her breadth — a proportion that others were to follow throughout the period. She had three galleries, the two uppermost linked by a row of windows, the essence of the decoration centring around the Prince of Wales' plumes motif as well as masks and swags and garlands, all picked out with white on gilt carving backed by green. The carving, gilding and elaborate painting alone cost over £1300 — a vast sum for the time, and more indicative of Stuart extravagance than of concern for fighting capabilities. But in this elaborate decoration, together with the figurehead at the beakhead, she was to prove a leader to all the great ships of her time. She was also, for practical reasons of strength, double-planked, 'and all the butt heads were double-bolted with iron bolts'.

As with other ships of her time and those to follow, the old boarding nets had been replaced by roofs of wooden grating over the deck, which would protect the guns' crews below from falling spars, blocks and rigging during gun actions. These also helped to allow the smoke from her own guns to disperse, and for this reason a number of planks in both the after or quarterdeck, as well as the forecastle, were also replaced by grating. This is indication enough, if such were needed, that sea battles had now turned into artillery fights afloat and that the old days of boarding were essentially over. Such actions on occasion continued right through the eighteenth and even the nineteenth centuries, but they were becoming rare. The last time when the call 'Out cutlasses and board!' was ever heard was probably in 1939, when the crew of the British destroyer *Cossack* came alongside the German-controlled merchantman *Altmark* in Norwegian waters.

The unequalled and visible example, of course, of a seventeenth century warship is the Swedish *Wasa* which now rests in the *Wasa* museum Stockholm, a source of historical interest to all concerned with old ships, and to everyone for the wealth of her carving, enabling us to see exactly how beautiful were many of the European ships of this century. She sank on 10 August 1628 while on her maiden voyage, being struck by a squall, dipping her gunports under water (like *Mary Rose)* and going straight to the bottom. With these visual images of memorable carving and gilding to help, one can more easily imagine the splendour of *Sovereign of the Seas* launched for Charles I in 1637. It must not be thought that *Sovereign* was in any way typical of her time or even of her class of ship. From the very beginning, under the eye of Phineas Pett and at the instigation of Charles I, she was intended to be the most powerful ship afloat, and the most glorious to look at. Her foes who encountered her in a number of seafights and other engagements during the Anglo-Dutch wars called her with some admiration 'The Golden Devil'. Throughout her life, the seventeenth century being indifferent to precision in the matter of names, she was referred to not only as *Sovereign of the Seas,* but as *Sovereign Royal, Royal Sovereign,* or just *Sovereign.* The expenditure on her building and decorating probably did as much as any individual thing to lead to those complaints about the king's heavy taxation of his subjects that finally cost him his head.

Sovereign was 127 feet long on the keel, 46.6 feet wide, and of uncertain draught although possibly as much as 22 feet. Again, estimates of her gross tonnage vary, for she suffered so many alterations over the years that the ship, as built for Charles I in 1637, had vastly altered in appearance by the time that she finally went up in flames nearly sixty years later in 1696 — not in action, but in a simple accident said to have arisen through a candle being accidentally knocked over. As to tonnage, there seems no doubt that she was about 400 tons larger than *Prince,* probably in the region of 1500 gross. At that time a 40 gun ship on average cost about £6000, but *Sovereign* with 100 guns finally costed out at £65,586 — most of this additional expense being incurred by her lavish appointments and her extraordinary wealth of carving and gilding. The royal master carver, Gerald Christmas, together with his sons and assistants is said to have carried out all this work, based on designs by Vandyke. Björn Landstrom describes them in *The Ship:*

The figurehead represented Edgar the Peaceful (!) riding down seven enemy kings. The beakhead railings were decorated with the greyhounds of Henry VII and the dragon of Cadwallader, with the lion and the unicorn, with the roses of England, the thistle of Scotland, the fleur de lis of France and the harp of Ireland, with royal monograms and various heraldic beasts. The forepost was topped with a cupid mounted on a lion, and two satyrs grinned from under the catheads on the forecastle. Between the satyrs the whole forepart of the forecastle was decorated with six beautiful goddesses symbolizing Counsel, Care, Industry, Strength, Valour and Victory. The sides were decorated with three friezes. The lowest was the simplest and consisted only of coats-of-arms and volutions. The central frieze, interrupted by the gunports, had helmets, cuirasses, musical instruments and all sorts of weapons. The upper which decorated the sides of the forecastle and half deck portrayed the Signs of the Zodiac alternating with representations of Roman Emperors. The galleries with their cupolas and long rows of windows were covered with mythological figures and scenes, royal coats of arms and monograms. The high stern was dominated by the Goddess of Victory surrounded by Neptune and Jupiter, Jason and Hercules. On either side of the rudder was the following inscription:

Qui mare, qui fluctus, ventos, navesque gubernat,
Sospitete hanc arcem, Carole magne, tuam.

Roughly meaning: May He whom sea and tides obey, and the winds that blow and the ships, Guard this, great Charles, thy man-of-war with sustenance Divine.

All this seems a far call from warships like *Revenge*. And yet the purpose was the same, and *Sovereign* took part in many a sea battle and was never defeated. It is doubtful also if the conditions of her sailors were any better than the Elizabethans, while the guns which they served were almost identical — indeed a little plainer, even if all cast in bronze. Van de Velde the Elder, who became so famous a marine painter, sketched this elaborate stern to show the work of art that it was — but the guns would have been quite familiar to earlier sailors and gunners. The gun ports had stayed the same size as before, two feet six inches square and, with the passing of the seventeenth century, the guns themselves became standardized. No longer ornamented like so many of those in *Mary Rose*, for instance, they were cast all in one piece, although the barrel was still reinforced by four rings or mouldings. These 32 pounders weighing about three tons had trunnions behind the second of these rings which fitted into bearings on the gun carriage, itself little changed from the first used in Henry VII's days, and to be seen to this day almost exactly as they remained over the centuries, aboard HMS *Victory*.

Handspikes were used to lever up the guns, a wedge-shaped block of wood being knocked in below the breech to hold it in place at the required angle, while equally primitive were the methods used to train the gun right or left, as far as was possible within the width of the gun port. Handspikes again were thrust beneath the carriage, exerting their leverage against the deck. Douglas G. Browne comments of this:

This crude use of handspikes did much damage to deck planking, and captains who put outward smartness before efficiency (a tendency that was to develop dangerously between Trafalgar and the War of 1812) made it an excuse to restrict gunnery practice. As long as all the 'machinery' of the ship had to be operated solely by man power very little would alter in hull design, in masting and rigging design — or in the guns themselves. For very many centuries the same static condition had been reached by the ancient shipbuilders in the Mediterranean Sea — to be changed only by the advent of gunpowder, and then by the efficient sail-driven warship.

Ship and boat builders have been constantly accused of being the most conservative of men: this being held against them in their own countries on the occasions when some new material, design or method of propulsion has been developed elsewhere. Their conservatism, however, is no stranger than that of the house builder ('Still using bricks and wooden window frames?') One distinct difference from their predecessors that will be noticed in *Sovereign* and other ships of her period and later is that the bonaventure mizzen has disappeared. In hull design the rounding of the stern, only flattening out some ten feet above the waterline, was new, and became a feature of English ships. Dutch and French retained the old flat stern. The three master is now, even for the very largest ships, the standard rig: alterations and improvements in sails and rigging being used to achieve greater efficiency and power. *Sovereign,* for instance, can set a topgallant sail on her mizzen over the topsail, and royals over her fore topgallant and her main topgallant. These royals were in advance of their time, and only came into general use in the mid-eighteenth century. They were peculiar to *Royal Sovereign* at this period, and it is for this reason that, when they were later and widely revived, they became known to seamen as 'royals'. There is some doubt as to whether her 'royals' were ever set, and indeed *Sovereign* initially proved as great a disaster as all her critics (both of her size and cost) had long prophesied she would be. It was not until her rig was reduced and a lot of her upperwork was cut down that she became — long after the execution of

Charles I — an efficient fighting ship. As originally conceived and launched it was soon found that she lay so deep in the water that the lower gun ports on the lee side could never be opened if she was even slightly heeled.

The Anglo-Dutch wars which occupy most naval attention throughout the seventeenth century, fought between two maritime nations equally familiar with the waters of the North Sea and the Channel, were made inevitable by trade rivalry and did not really begin until, curiously enough, England like Holland had also become a republic. Oliver Cromwell himself paid a great deal of attention to the navy and much new building took place during the Commonwealth period. What emerged from the many engagements between English and Dutch was the triumph of the broadside and with it the line ahead as the ideal battle formation. Needless to say, it was rarely achieved, and indeed the Dutch often preferred to fight in individual squadrons, while the over-large size of the fleets on both sides and the fact that first, second and third rate sized ships were indiscriminately mixed precluded any organized system of tactics from being firmly developed. Indeed, many of the battles, however formally they began, tended to end up in mixed mêlées where ship fought against ship, or small groups against one another. Dutch ship building at this time was probably superior to English and as a sea power Holland often showed herself superior to her enemy. It is noticeable that when Cardinal Richlieu was building up the new navy of France it was to Holland that he turned for the building of the first new great ships for his king. A surprising factor of these Anglo-Dutch wars is that whereas the Dutch had admirals in command of their fleets the English had gone back to the bad old habit of placing their command in the hands of nobly born soldiers, or 'generals at sea'. Pepys tells of how he heard the wife of Monck, the Duke of Albemarle (himself 'general at sea'), 'cry mightily out against the having of gentlemen captains, with feathers and ribbons, and wish the King (Charles II) would send her husband to sea with the plain old sea-captains that he served with formerly.'

The Restoration clearly had done nothing to stop these out of date absurdities: the only great difference was that the 'Black Boy', with all his extravagances and dissolute Court, had a real regard for ships and the sea (which his father had not) and also that he had the great good fortune to have Mr Pepys among others at the Admiralty. A successor of Pepys, in the reign of Queen Anne, remarked in a letter to the then Lord High Admiral that however the reign of Charles II may have been exploded for other things, it cannot be so in relation to the navy, 'for His Majesty's care extended no less to the officering the fleet with able seamen than to the maintenance of it with good husbandry.' Despite the great and famous disaster (for the English) when the Dutch under de Ruyter blockaded the Thames and raided Chatham, peace was finally signed by the two warring nations at Breda in 1667. The peace was necessitated largely for the Dutch by their geographical position, for it was clear that despite her successes Holland could not indefinitely stand the permanent threat to her trade and livelihood that was entailed by a hostile English fleet in command of the Channel. Both sides kept their conquests made in the wars, England thus obtaining New York and New Jersey. Prior to de Ruyter's great Chatham raid, which served to give the Dutch the bargaining card to conclude a peace, there had been a very typical series of engagements, sometimes known as the battle of the Gunfleet since part of the action took place near the Gunfleet Sands off the mouth of the Thames.

On June 29 1666 de Ruyter had put to sea to blockade the Thames with a fleet of over a hundred ships, being the usual mixture of both great and small, with van Tromp and Jan Evertszoon also in command. With their considerable seamanship and the use of those small shallow draught vessels in which they specialized (and with which they had so greatly helped to defeat the Armada by stopping Parma from any invasion attempt) they managed to halt all the trade of London; their light craft scudding in and out of the shallows and sandbanks of the Thames mouth while their main fleet lay off the Essex coast. It is significant that, together with over seventy line-of-battle ships and twenty-six frigates, the Dutch had with them twenty light craft for use as fireships: in these seventeenth century wars fireships often played a major part. The English fleet under Monck, Duke of Albermarle, and Prince Rupert, dashing cavalry commander of the Civil War, as second in command, numbered over eighty fighting ships of various rates, together also with a squadron of fireships. Among the fighting ships was the brand new *Loyal London,* commissioned that year and straight from the Chatham yard. A 96 gun three decker, she was one of a new type of smaller three decker and was financed by the City of London as part of their contribution to the war effort. One hundred and twenty-five feet on the keel and some 40 on the beam, she was almost as powerful as a 100-gun first rate; thus, as often happens over the centuries, types of ships begin to blend with one another so that it is sometimes difficult to ascribe a definite class to them. (For instance, in the late twentieth century we have 'destroyers' of five or six thousand tons, whereas in World War II such would have been called cruisers, even if light cruisers. And of course their firepower no longer bears much relation to their tonnage.) In general it was found, however, by both English and Dutch that the large two decker was the best type of warship.

Having mustered his fleet in the lower Thames, Monck was faced with the problem of getting it out in the face of the enemy, for there was no way through the narrow deep channels save line ahead — with the grave danger that as they emerged one by one, the van might easily be destroyed by a united waiting force. He must endeavour to bring out the whole fleet on a fast ebbing tide with a fair wind behind them. This he managed to do on 22 July, the experienced Thames pilots bringing out a whole powerful battle fleet without a single ship touching ground. A few Dutch ships on lookout off the edge of the Gunfleet Sands withdrew as a squadron of nine ships of the line headed by one with the famous name *Revenge*, together with fireships, made to attack them. It was too late in the day for a major action to develop and de Ruyter held back to seaward while the whole English fleet anchored off the Gunfleet.

The expected action did not develop the following day because an uneasy calm fell, to be followed towards sunset by a typical summer thunder storm in the course of which the only casualty of this protracted overture was *Jersey* which was struck by lightning, so badly damaging her rigging that she had to leave the English fleet on the following dawn. The next day Monck found that the Dutch had completely withdrawn, de Ruyter wisely heading seaward until more settled conditions of wind and weather enabled him to work out his tactics. It was not until the 25th, again with only a light wind ruffling the grey North Sea, that both sides were able to come into action.

In the formalized convention of the day (which would seem to have evolved into military fashion, like the old actions of Mediterranean galleys) both sides were disposed into three parts the van, the centre and the rear. Jan Evertszoon commanded the Dutch van, de Ruyter their centre, and van Tromp their rear. On the English side the van was led by Sir Thomas Allen, the centre by Monck and Prince Rupert, and the rear by Sir Jeremy Smith. The English at this time divided their fleets according to this formal battle array into white ensign for the van (now the ensign of the Royal Navy), red ensign for the centre (now the merchant marine) and blue ensign for the rear (now fleet auxiliaries and the like). In this systematized warfare — so reminiscent of the 'quadrilles' of galleys and so far removed from the individualistic Elizabethan style — it was expected that van should encounter van; centre, centre; and rear, rear. (In practice, of course, things never quite worked out as intended, but the formalism of such naval battles is perfectly represented in some of the great Dutch paintings of the time.)

Action began early in the morning, but so light was the wind that there was little or no scope for manoeuvring, the two fleets drifting slowly together, Monck in *Royal Charles* engaging de Ruyter's *Seven Provinces* and fighting a long gun duel together, just as others were doing; casualties on both sides were heavy, both sides showing that similar dogged endurance which was typical of their somewhat similar national characters. Both sides also attempted to break the deadlock by the use of fireships, the Dutch scoring the only success, the old *Prince Royal* (built 1641) being set alight and drifting onto a sandbank where she was abandoned and burned to the water's edge.

In London the gunfire could be heard throughout a sultry July afternoon, people listening to its distant rumble with the fearful anxiety of all those who over the centuries and in many places have listened to the sound of invisible battles that may determine their fates. Pepys had gone to Whitehall but found that since it was St James's Day the Court were at chapel and so, 'we waiting chapel being done, come people out of the park, telling us that guns are heard plainly. And so everybody to the park, and by and by the chapel done, the King and the Duke into the bowling-green and upon the leads, whither I went, and there the guns were plain to be heard....'

With even the slight wind falling towards sunset, both sides had drifted into what almost amounted to two separate engagements — hard slogging and no chance to manoeuvre. Darkness and calm ended the day. On the 26th there was calm again, and no action was possible except for a typical diversion in cavalier manner by Prince Rupert who sailed his small yacht under the stern of de Ruyter's flagship (where there were no guns to reply) and fired his miniature cannon into the Dutchman's grand and gilded stern — running rapidly for cover when an errant puff of air began to turn the flagship where a broadside (or one cannon even) could have blown him out of the water. Both sides spent the day repairing damage to structure, rigging and sails while transferring their wounded to light craft that could take them home, whether to England or Holland.

That night came the first wind of what became 'the four day battle' and de Ruyter decided on withdrawal. He had, after all, achieved a tactical victory in holding up the trade of London, showing to that city and to others on the coast how vulnerable they were to Dutch sea power. Ragged running battles took place during the following day as the Dutch made for the security of their own coast, with the English on their heels. Some later English historians have liked to claim the whole affair as 'a substantial victory' but it is difficult to see it as such — a success, maybe, since the blockade of the Thames mouth had been broken and the Dutch finally forced to withdraw into the North Sea and make for their home ports. But in many ways it was typical of such seventeenth-century actions between these two evenly matched forces, both with somewhat similar ships, equally well based in knowledge of their home seas, and equally imbued with stubborn courage.

Out of the somewhat inconclusive Anglo-Dutch wars there emerged one definite conclusion: the mixed line of battle, the hodge-podge in which ships of varying sizes and weight of guns sailed and fought together, was as unsuitable a mixture as Mediterranean admirals had earlier found the combination of sailing ships and oar-propelled vessels. At that time there were the large first rates of over ninety to one hundred guns, the second rates of over seventy to ninety guns, and the third rates of sixty to seventy guns. It was the latter class that was to emerge triumphant for overall usage. It was not only a question of money; third rates had shown themselves more versatile, their lighter draught giving them many an advantage, easier to handle and nimbler, and at the same time heavily enough gunned — especially when used in groups together — to cope with almost any circumstances. In fact, what was to some extent repeated was the earlier triumph of ships like *Revenge* as compared with *Great Harry*. First rates continued to be built, but to some extent more as a form of insurance against the enemy suddenly producing a battleship. They were also of course emblems of national and royal pride.

Sir Anthony Deane's *Doctrine of Naval Architecture*, which was among Pepy's contemporary manuscripts, contains mast and rigging plans for six rates of ships as well

as body plans, among which is the first known example of
one of these third rates which were to prove so important
in the future. Ship building had, at long last, come within
the disciplines of the professional. Among Deane's body
plans, the third rate is the earliest example found in England
of a plan showing a draught complete enough accurately
to define the shape of the ship. One general trend both in
English and Dutch ship building during this period was
the shortening of the beak, at the same time widening it
and setting it at a much higher angle. This was because,
especially in smaller vessels like the third rates, the old long
low beak became very 'wet' in anything like a sea, while
the lower forecastle also called for more harmonious lines
in the eyes of naval architects, as well as seamen. Another
improvement was in the method of sheathing ships against
fouling and especially the dreaded teredo worm to be met
in warm waters. Earlier methods had been to cover the
underwater body of the ship with a layer of tar, sulphur
and tallow after her building, and then to affix expendable
planking. In 1670 Anthony Deane first sheathed *Phoenix,* a
fourth rate, with milled lead sheeting fastened with copper
or iron bolts. This type of sheathing was used on new third
rates that were building as well as lesser rates, but its cost
was high and in the long run it was found that electrolytic
action took place between the fastenings and those of the
hull. The solution to underwater fouling was not found until
the discovery of the use of copper for the purpose in the
eighteenth century, but it became more and more important
as ships like third rates were required to stay at sea for long
periods and in various waters. The fact that, from about the
time of the Restoration onwards, it became the practice in
England to have models made of important ships about to
be built — for submission both to the Admiralty and to the
king — meant that from then on the changes in shipbuilding
are well recorded as well as in architectural plans. A fine
early model, now in the Science Museum London, shows
the 100-gun *Prince* (1670) which conveys the impression far
better than any words can do of a great ship of the late

seventeenth century. A model believed to be *Loyal London,* which took part in the Gunfleet engagement, can also be seen.

While these main developments of the great warship were going on it must not be forgotten that, in the Mediterranean, the galley and the galleasse still predominated. The two great powers which had both Atlantic and Mediterranean coastlines, France and Spain, were naturally compelled to keep two different types of ship. They continued to have oared navies until well into the eighteenth century as did the Knights of St John who, from their small fortress island of Malta, maintained their incessant warfare against the Moslem powers for centuries after the new nations of Europe had forgotten all about the Crusades. The corsairs of the Barbary coast, operating from such 'pirate states' as Algiers and Tripoli, continued ceaselessly to harry European merchant shipping (most of the powers being more prepared to pay a kind of 'Dane geld' than do anything about it). The Italian maritime states, however, as well as the Knights and France, had still to protect their shipping and their coastlines against the fast Moslem corsairs who under sail and oar made life permanently hazardous upon the sea.

French naval galleys of the seventeenth century generally divided into two classes: *ordinary* having 26 pairs of thwarts, and *extraordinary* with 33 pairs. Usually there were five oarsmen to a thwart so that the total number on an *ordinary* was 260 men. Sailors, soldiers, gunners and officers were of course all in addition to this basic complement. The largest of all these oar-propelled vessels were the 'royal' galleys of France, the flagship of the French galley fleet being always called *La Réale* and flying the flag of the king as well as that of the galley commander. In the Musee de la Marine in Paris the carving which decorated the stern of one of these, executed by Pierre Puget the sculptor, can still be seen and Björn Landstrom, working from contemporary drawings, has managed to reconstruct it: about 170 feet on the waterline and 21 feet wide, it had 31 pairs of thwarts. The galley slave crew alone would have been 427 and this 'royal' also carried two lateen sails, giving it about 8000 square feet of canvas when under sail. It still suffered, however, from the galley's main fault in the new age — lack of firepower. Light swivel guns were mounted on the catwalks outboard of the oarsmen, but as always its main armament was all forward: the largest gun, a 36-pounder being mounted in the centre of the forward fighting platform with two 24-pounders and then two 18-pounders outboard of it.

For the reasons given above, such vessels continued to hold a place in Mediterranean history until the eighteenth century, the last French 'royal' being built in 1720. The threat from the Barbary pirates continued, however, right up to the advent of the Age of Steam and it was a power from the New World, the American navy, which was largely responsible for routing out the last of them. Hence the words in the American marines' song 'From the halls of Montezuma to the shores of Tripoli...' for it was Captain Bainbridge and Stephen Decatur at the head of a squadron who finally broke the power of the infamous Pashas of Tripoli. The recent history of this part of the North African coast has shown an unpleasant recrudescence of the old spirit.

CHAPTER SIX

The Ship of the Line and Frigates

The eighteenth century and beyond was dominated by the wars between France and England, so it is natural that the development of the greatest fighting ships of the time should be looked for among these two powers. Spain was in decline though capable of good shipbuilding as she would show as an ally of France; Holland contented herself with her overseas empire and, like a sensible trader, kept as aloof as possible from the fray. The Mediterranean world was quiet save for the corsairs, or the occasions when the two great warring powers involved themselves on its waters, while the other great powers of the future had not yet arisen. In the north, however, Peter the Great, Tsar of all the Russias, had already clearly signalled his intentions for his country: 'I am not looking for land, I am looking for water.'

As the English were to find out, during that long series of protracted wars, the ships built in French dockyards, and indeed often in those of Spain, were definitely superior to their own. In England the master shipwrights at the royal dockyards dominated the scene, and the mathematicians and architects, whose talents had at one time seemed as if they could find employment in the design and construction of ships, were to turn their attentions elsewhere; while the same conservative group (family even succeeding family at the royal dockyards) continued to work in the methods that had been deplored by Captain Weymouth in the seventeenth century. Added to this, as Oppenheim mentions '...the system that made it to each man's pecuniary interest to

obtain as many ships as possible to build and repair, and
to exert all his personal influence to that end, converted the
dockyards into nests of intrigue.'

In Europe, on the contrary, and even as far afield as
Russia, improvements in design and in almost every aspect
of shipbuilding were taking place under the new spirit
of scientific inquiry fathered so largely by France. The
complacency and native conservatism of the English yards
would hardly be shaken until a new spirit was forced upon
them by the harsh facts of war, and it still remains true
that as late as the Napoleonic wars the English were always
happy if they could capture a French ship because more
often than not she would prove to be better in all respects
than one of their own of a similar class. On the other hand,
as the century advanced, one thing became apparent, that
the days in England where, as we have seen, high sea-going
commands were given to prominent soldiers and men of
noble blood had gone. There was a reversion to the far
more sensible outlook of the Elizabethan period and the
emergence of men who had risen to the top without military
honours or court influence, but who were seamen first and
foremost. The French navy, however, until the Revolution
(which for a time almost destroyed it), was officered in
much the same way as the Spanish had been in the days
of the Armada. While their ships were the best in the
world their senior officers came from the court circle, with
all the limitations that entailed. The British, on the other
hand, were constrained by the rigid code of 'The Fighting
Instructions for the Navy', first drawn up by the Duke of
York (later James II) when he was Lord High Admiral.

These were designed to provide a set pattern according
to which naval engagements should be conducted and, even
allowing for the wisdom based on acquired knowledge
of many of them, they tended to lay a dead head upon all
commanders. Above all they contemplated a formal set piece
battle where both fleets in line ahead passed and repassed
each other on opposite tacks, exchanging broadsides. The
line must never be broken, nor any ship retire without the

admiral's permission, and — since the French adopted almost similar tactics — battles became formal duels. Only if one line or other were to be reduced to disorder and a flight began could the line be broken, and the signal made for a general chase. As can be imagined a great many of the naval battles of this century ended in what was more or less a stalemate: both sides afterwards claiming a victory and the whole record, from the historian's point of view, making dull reading.

One significant difference between the two navies was the style of firing, the English — just as they had done in Armada times — tending to concentrate on the enemy's hull (hitting him 'between wind and water'), while the French aimed for masts and rigging, in the hope of crippling their adversary, thus compelling him to break the line by falling out of it. The earlier important distinction between having the weather gauge or not had largely disappeared owing to the strict formalism of such actions, its only advantage now being that it might compel the enemy to an action that, for whatever reason, he might be anxious to avoid. French admirals, in fact, often preferred the leeward position for (not being rigidly bound by the same fighting instructions as their opponents) they could turn their ships away if need be, relying also on the fact that their ships were almost certainly faster than those of the English — who in any case could not pursue unless their admiral had signalled the general chase. It was not until bolder spirits arose on both sides that close, decisive fighting once again changed the long and wearingly formal pattern of naval warfare that had existed for a century. Over and over again in accounts of these battles one is reminded of long drawn-out chess matches between champions of almost identical ability — the whole pattern of the game finally reaching a kind of stasis, which it required some genius to come along and shatter.

This was indeed to happen, and it was to be foreshadowed by the action of Rodney in 1782 off the West Indian island of Dominica, the battle of the Saintes.

When, due to a sudden change of wind, a gap opened

in the French line immediately opposite Rodney's flagship
it was his right-hand man, Sir Charles Douglas, who first
proposed to him that they should push through the line
cutting off the French rear from the van. With the rest of the
line following his flagship Rodney would be able to destroy
the French rear before the French admiral, de Grasse, could
come about to its aid. Rodney at first demurred but then,
seeing the eminent wisdom of Douglas's suggestion, headed
for the gap with other ships (their captains no doubt more
than perplexed) following him. The decisive victory that
followed justified Rodney's action — which was lucky
indeed for him, since disgrace and ruin would have been
his if he had not succeeded. He had, after all, broken the
sixteenth of those sacrosanct 'Fighting Instructions': 'In
all cases of fight with the enemy the commanders of His
Majesty's ships are to *keep the fleet in one line,* and (as
much as may be) to preserve that order of battle, which they
have been directed to keep before the time of fight.' (In this
particular case, Admiral Rodney himself had hoisted the
signal to 'fight to leeward' of the French. When, following
Douglas's suggestion, he had changed his mind and turned
aside, his flagship *Formidable* was still flying this forgotten
signal.)

During this period of the 'establishments', in which the
standard dimensions of each class of warship were laid
down, both English and French gradually worked towards
a similar pattern of building, but 'French preeminence in
design', as Laird Clowes has pointed out, 'became even
more definite', and, 'the origin or nearly every one of our
improved types can be traced to some French prize'. Given
this fact, what finally emerged was six rates of warship
forming the battle fleet. The lowest of these, the sixth rate,
mounted 28 guns, after which came the fifth rate, mounting
between 36 and 44 guns. Both of these were ship-rigged,
called frigates, and provided those 'eyes of the fleet' — for
which Nelson was often to call in vain, when engaged on
one of his attempts to find the French and bring them to
battle. Fourth rates, which were gradually to disappear

or be phased out towards the end of the century, as being neither quite one thing nor another, were 50 gun ships. As the frigate gained in importance and as the French and Spanish tended to build theirs both larger and better than the British they became more and more important in all navies, some of this class late in the century even having as many as 40 guns. The third rate was to become during the Napoleonic wars the maid of all work, carrying between 64 and 80 guns, but with the 74-gun ships emerging in both navies as predominant (there were fifteen 74s out of 27 ships in Nelson's fleet at Trafalgar). They were two-decked warships, whereas frigates were single-decked, and the class above them, the second rates, were three deckers. These mounted 90 guns and had a complement of about 700 men. Finally, at the top of the list, came the great ship herself, the first rate, mounting 100 guns and more on three decks, with a complement of about 850 seamen, marines, and officers. An important if miscellaneous group attached to any fleet were such vessels as bomb ketches, sloops of war, cutters, schooners and fire ships.

The climactic battle of this whole period of the great sailing warship was of course that of Trafalgar on 21 October 1805. It is also the best known — principally because it established British naval supremacy on the high seas for over a century and also because it was the climax of Nelson's career and ended in his death. It contributed largely towards the defeat of Napoleon's schemes for the invasion of England and his ambitions on the continent of Europe, although of course these were not terminated until 18 June 1815 at Waterloo. Trafalgar, however, was in some respects hardly as interesting as the battle of the Nile, 1798, which dissolved Napoleonic dreams in the East, and which was supreme tactically as well as being one of the most complete of victories in all naval history. Copenhagen, on the other hand, was the hardest fought of all and must continue to interest the student of the great wooden built sailing warship since it was fought mainly against fortified land positions and large well prepared hulks, that had themselves been

turned into floating forts. The ability of the great ship built
of wood to absorb punishment as well as hand it out was
hardly ever better revealed than at Copenhagen. But, well
known though it is, it remains Trafalgar which must later be
briefly considered since, both as to tactics and the behaviour
of great ships in action, it marks the culmination of an era
that had begun so many centuries before. Steam, which was
on the horizon, would ultimately provide the motive power
to dispossess the sailing warship as effectively as the latter
had dispossessed the oar-propelled galley.

As the sole existing first rate, as the sole great ship
and representative of a whole era, *Victory* would have
an immediate claim on the attention even if she had not
attained eternal fame as Nelson's flagship at Trafalgar.
Quite apart from the fact that nearly half a million people
visit her annually in her dry dock in Portsmouth, *Victory*
would still be one of the most famous ships in history even
if, like Drake's *Golden Hind,* she had completely vanished.
She was designed by Sir William Slade, one of the greatest
British naval architects, and a man who in company with
others began a breakthrough in the science that served to
pull the country back from the torpor into which it had
declined, and to recapture the spirit that had for quite some
time animated French ship design and building. In his time
Slade was remarkable for being the designer of most of
those all important early 74-gun ships, as well as a number
of the early frigates, the first rate *Victory* being the peak of
a brilliant career. Even in his lifetime she was regarded as
his masterpiece and she was the only opportunity that Slade
ever had to build a 100-gun ship.

These had declined slightly in numbers during the
eighteenth century, and a new first rate was at that time as
rare a commision as a new battleship during the inter-war
period of the twentieth century in any European country.
Two new first rates had been built on the 1745 establishment,
and it was not until 1758 that Slade received the order from
the Admiralty for a new 100-gun ship. First rates were
normally built in a dock and then 'floated up' when their

time came, and the same rule applied to *Victory,* whose keel was laid in the old Single Dock at the Royal Dockyard, Chatham, on 23 July 1759. It was not, however, until May 1765 that she was launched.

Her keel was a 150 foot length of English elm, 20 inches square, and was formed of seven trunks. Her greatest width was 51.5 feet. The ribs and planking were of oak, and it is probably the length of time taken in her completion — more than twice the amount of years normally required for a first rate — which enabled her (even allowing for refits) to last so long. (The practice of 'standing in frame', allowing timbers to weather and to betray any decay before planking and completion was a very important one.) Of 2162 tons, carrying 104 guns, *Victory* was manned by 850 officers and men. On the lower gun decks of first rates at the time that she first came into commission the largest class of gun — the 42-pounder was to be found. The disadvantage of its slower rate of fire as compared with the 32-pounder was already becoming apparent, and it is significant that *Victory's* first admiral, the Honourable Augustus Keppel, who hoisted his flag in her in April 1778, asked for the 42-pounders to be replaced with 32-pounders. As she was armed in the days of her great renown, she had thirty 12-pounders on the upper gun deck, twenty-eight 24-pounders on her middle gun deck, and thirty 32-pounders on her lower gun deck. The cannon on the upper gun deck had a total weight of 52 tons, the middle gun deck 70 tons, and the lower gun deck 84 tons. On the half deck she carried two 12-pounders, and on the forecastle deck two 12-pounders and two 68-pounder *carronades*. The latter were powerful, short-range guns taking their name from the town of Carron in Scotland where they were first made by the local iron company. A short barrelled gun with a small charge but a large shot, it had been suggested that it would serve well at close quarter work — where many actions were fought in any case. (As *Victory* passed under the stern of the French flagship, *Bucentaure* at Trafalgar, she fired her port side *carronade* straight through the enemy's stern windows to terrible effect.)

Something else that was introduced at about the same
time as the *carronade,* after *Victory* had seen some years'
service, was coppering. During the Anglo-French wars so
much of the service was seen in the warm waters of the West
Indies where shipworm was rife and weed growth extremely
dense, the advantages of coppering were seen to outweigh
the expense. Earlier attempts at the use of thin copper sheets
for this purpose had been abandoned because the electrolytic
action set up between the copper and the fastenings of the
hull were unacceptable. Then, in the late 1770s, it was
considered that a thick layer of paper affixed by tar to the
hull, and serving as a barrier between the copper sheets and
the iron fastenings of the latter, would serve the purpose (a
technique still used in small wooden-hulled boats with iron
fastenings right into the twentieth century). In the long term,
however, it was found that the only complete answer was to
make the fastenings of the hull out of a mixture of copper
and zinc. In the meantime, Royal Naval vessels benefited on
oceanic crossings and in the waters of warm seas from this
protection against worm, as well as its delaying effect on
weed growth.

Victory first saw action in 1778 following the French
Treaty affording recognition to the American Colonies,
which led to a state of war between Britain and France. The
action was inconclusive, *Victory* suffering some damage
aloft to rigging and spars. Already though, as with that
other earlier great ship, *Mary Rose,* she had proved as fast
and quick to handle as a vessel of a smaller class than her
own. (Nelson will have first seen her when she lay still
untried and in reserve in 1771, when he joined *Raisonable*
at Chatham as a midshipman aged 12 years and 3 months.)
Victory was at sea until the close of 1782, and then after a
refit went into reserve following a peace that lasted with a
few alarms of war until 1789. It was not really until 1793
when, wearing the flag of Admiral Lord Hood, *Victory* after
so very many years began a life of action that was hardly to
cease throughout the whole period of the Napoleonic wars,
including much time in the Mediterranean, the inevitable

blockading actions of French ports, and in 1797 the battle of Cape St Vincent. Wearing the flag of Admiral Sir John Jervis, she led the fleet of 15 British ships of the line and achieved a formidable victory over 27 similar Spanish warships and a number of other heavily-armed ships forming a convoy. It was the greatest naval engagement since the day when Rodney had broken the line at the battle of the Saintes in 1782. It is significant that this was the day when Nelson in the 74-gun *Captain* also left the line, in disobedience of the 'Fighting Instructions', and in doing so captured two large Spanish warships, one of them being the Spanish's admiral's. Peter Whitlock in his history of *Victory* describes her expensive refit in 1803:

> The stern galleries were removed and the stern enclosed; the figurehead was changed to the simple attractive royal coat of arms she wore at Trafalgar; shot racks and gun ports were altered; a gaff fitted to the mizzen instead of the old lateen yard; the magazines were lined with copper to prevent the entry of rats, which gnawed their way in then trailed powder from their coats around the ship; a sick bay was fitted in the bow to improve the lot of the sick as opposed to the wounded, and Nelson, who was now going to take her as his flagship, ordered the quarter deck skylight to be decked in to improve deck space between the quarterdeck 12-pounder guns. The main armament now consisted of thirty 32-pounder flintlock guns — probably the first of the first rates so fitted.

Sir Charles Douglas, the same who had been Rodney's right hand man at the battle of the Saintes, was a gunnery expert and it was he who had been largely responsible for the substitution in the navy of flintlocks and priming tubes for the old powder horns and portfires. An alteration in *Victory's* rig was from the lateen on the mizzen to the more easily managed gaff (probably first originating with the Dutch), the lateen spar itself being retained aboard as a spare in the event of others being damaged in action. Noticeable

also was a change that took place towards the close of
the eighteenth century in many two and three deckers —
the closing of the stern. The open stern galleries had long
disclosed a want of strength at this point aft, but had been
retained because of their understandable popularity with
senior officers. *Victory* shows an excellent example of this
conversion (and *Bucentaure* in the Trafalgar action was
to show its weaknesses). Nevertheless, flag officers being
a demanding breed, stern walks appeared again in the
nineteenth century and, even with all the modifications of
steel, were still found in some capital ships as late as World
War II.

Admiral Villeneuve, who as a rear admiral with the
French expeditionary force had probably awaited the attack
of the British with complete confidence at the battle of the
Nile, had no such reason to feel similarly at Trafalgar. He
had been forced out of Cadiz along with the Spanish fleet
on Napoleon's orders, although he knew well that the fleet
under his command was not ready for action. In terms of
numbers, however, he had more than enough to give battle
to the British when they hove in sight — and numbers
probably counted more for a military man like the Emperor
than they did with an experienced seaman like Villeneuve,
who knew that discipline, training and the state of the
ships are as important as the health of the man at sea. His
orders were to proceed from Cadiz into the Mediterranean
in order to lend support to Napoleon's movements against
Austria and he hoped to pass through the Straits avoiding
any major action. Aware, however, that this might not be
possible (knowing how well the British kept watch and
ward) he had posted a reserve squadron under the Spanish
Admiral Gravina to keep to windward of the rest of the
fleet. He suspected that, if it was Nelson who should come
across him, the latter would very probably try and obtain
superiority over a part of his fleet. (In this had lain his
distinction in other actions — always with cool disregard of
those 'Fighting Instructions').

Nelson had indeed drawn up orders for his officers

explaining how he intended to fight the battle and they are contained in the well known 'Nelson Memorandum', drawn up at a time when in fact he expected to have a good many more than twenty seven ships in his company. Briefly and explicitly, they were that the British fleet would attack in two bodies. The larger, under Collingwood, was to obtain superiority over the enemy's rear (as Villeneuve had suspected), while the smaller, under Nelson, was to attack and keep away the van and the centre should they attempt to go to the assistance of their rear.

Soon after dawn on 20 October the French and Spanish fleet began to leave Cadiz harbour, their intention being to stand to the westward until all the ships were out and clear. Their fleet was composed of three divisions, the fourth under the Spanish admiral taking the windward station, to try and drive off the shadowing British frigates (too late), and themselves to act as lookouts for the British fleet. They were thus used much like a combination of cruisers and destroyers in later wars.

Villeneuve's fleet itself had been carefully mixed between French and Spanish ships so that the French could keep an eye on their allies, for there existed between the dominant partner and the other the same suspicion that exists between most allies in all wars.

21 October was a fair day after previous thick and rainy weather, the wind light from the north west, and the Allied fleet was now committed to their southward course for the Straits. Throughout the previous long hours while they had all got out from Cadiz Nelson had carefully kept his own fleet out of sight below the horizon, though its eyes were visible every now and then, wheeling and dipping on the edge of sight — those frigates without which in those days a fleet would have been as blind as a modern one deprived of all sensing and communicating mechanisms. When about twelve miles to the west of the Allied fleet Nelson ordered his ships to form the two lines as outlined in his plan; he himself leading the one and Collingwood in *Royal Sovereign* the other. With the light wind behind them the British also had

the further advantage that — the enemy lying to the west — their line was clearly visible at dawn, before Villeneuve could see the threatening columns approaching from the west.

On sighting the British, Villeneuve realized that he had underestimated the number that might be waiting for him and he now made a mistake of judgement, ordering the Spanish Admiral Gravina to join him with the reserve squadron. He thus sacrificed the one original part of his dispositions, and he compounded this error by ordering his fleet to wear and head back north so as to have Cadiz available for shelter when the clearly unavoidable action took place. In doing this he not only showed his own anxious uncertainty but also caused his fleet to execute a complicated manoeuvre (it took nearly two hours) in a light wind which was almost certainly to leave them in indifferent order. A long swell that had been ominously building up, while the wind still remained variable and light, suggested to all familiar with the area that a hard blow would follow on its heels. Nelson, remembering how Hawke had saved the British fleet by anchoring immediately after the action at Quiberon Bay (when the French had suffered disaster from a gale) had the hoist made 'Prepare to anchor after the close of day'. So the British approached in their two attacking lines, their speed never exceeding about two knots, even with studding sails set — something never before known for a fleet going into action. The results of the day are too familiar to need repeating: Collingwood brilliantly executed Nelson's orders, breaking through the rear to cut off the last twelve ships. In fact, he cut off the last fifteen, while Nelson's column, also advancing in irregular line ahead, burst through the centre which had become strung out and cut off twelve ships as he passed under the stern of *Bucentaure*. Most of the ships following him deployed to starboard and broke through the Allied fleet at various points between Nelson and Collingwood. With the enemy's backbone broken, the mêlée which Nelson had hoped to provoke then ensued, out of which the British gained the victory, with twenty prizes taken for only one British lost. Superior gunnery may be given the credit for much of this, once the initial superiority of Nelson's tactics is accepted. The Allied fleet had room to manoeuvre and a friendly port under their lee, but were so taken aback by the style of the attack and the way in which their fleet had been split that they had lost all coherence in their response. It was certainly not want of courage for, as Captain Blackwood of the frigate *Euryalus* wrote: 'They waited the attack of the British with a coolness I was sorry to witness. And they fought in a way that must do them honour.'

Although against a larger fleet, the British had the advantage in that they had been honed by long days at sea, whereas the French and the Spanish had been cooped up in port where they could not, for instance, even get in the very necessary gunnery practice that might have made a difference. The weakest point of Nelson's plan (a calculated risk) was the time incurred while his two arrowheads were approaching the Allied fleet when — theoretically — each leading ship should have been sunk by the combined gunfire of the long curved line of Spanish and French, the successors being equally dealt with as they in their turn came up to take the lead. Certainly both Nelson's *Victory* and Collingwood's *Royal Sovereign* did pass through a great storm of shot during the period while they led the approach, *Victory* being at least twenty minutes within range before she could return a single shot, but it was neither heavy enough nor skilfully enough directed, and once the British had got amongst the Allied fleet their disciplined, quicker rate of fire carried the day. For over a century the French with their faster ships had always been able to disengage from battles with the greater part of their fleet more or less intact, thus accounting for the numerous inconclusive engagements that had baffled the British. Nelson had brilliantly solved the problem of how to stop this happening, a fact which gives Trafalgar its immense distinction among all naval battles. From his own point of view he had to some extent failed at Trafalgar for, as from the Battle of the Nile onwards, he had

introduced into naval warfare a new and terrible conception
— the battle of annihilation.

A very curious fact of history, marking the last great fleet
action fought under sail, is that it happened in much the
same area as it had all begun. Prevaza, where Barbarossa
had encountered the great *Galleon of Venice,* lay not far to
the north, while Lepanto, scene of the last all-galley great sea
battle, was even closer. On 20 October 1827, at Navarino
on the south-west coast of Greece, in the great sandy bay of
Pylos, a fleet of somewhat unlikely allies — British, French
and Russian — under the command of Admiral Sir Edward
Codrington destroyed a mixed Turkish and Egyptian fleet.
This did more for the cause of Greek Independence than
had the death of Byron in marshy Missolonghi or all the
activities of European politicians. The fact that Codrington
precipitated this attack on the Ottoman Empire entirely on
his own initiative shows the latitude that was then allowed
to a British admiral overseas. The fact that the French and
Russians willingly accompanied him shows how great was
the international prestige of the Royal Navy. Apart from
being the last great engagement fought under sail, it was
also the last in which all the guns used were still smooth
bore. In a sense it was also the swansong of the old Royal
Navy, Codrington himself having served under Nelson at
Trafalgar. In the eighty-seven years that would elapse before
the British would fight another major battle at sea the
whole face of warfare, of ships, and indeed of everything
else throughout the planet, would have been changed by the
industrial revolution.

Although the lives of sailors and personal records of
naval actions have no part in this account of the great ship,
the memoirs of an anonymous British sailor (*Life on Board
a Man of War, 1829*) may serve as an epitaph to the whole
age — as well as a reminder of the horrors encapsulated in
those four words 'a battle took place'.

Lieutenant Broke drew his sword and told us not to fire

until ordered. 'Point your guns, sure, men,' he said, 'and make every shot tell — that's the way to show them British play!' He now threw away his hat on the deck, and told us to give the Turks three cheers, which we did with all our heart. Then crying out, 'Stand clear of the guns,' he gave the word 'FIRE!' and immediately the whole tier of guns was discharged, with terrific effect, into the side of the Turkish Admiral's ship that lay abreast of us.... The first man that I saw killed in our vessel was a marine, and it was not until we had received five or six rounds from the enemy. He was close beside me. I had taken the sponge out of his hand, and on turning round saw him at my feet with his head fairly severed from his body, as if it had been done with a knife. My messmate Lee drew the corpse out from the trucks of the guns, and hauled it into midships, under the after ladder.... As there is always a cask of water lashed to the stanchion in midships, called 'fighting water', one of the officers of the fore part of the deck, on his way to the cockpit, came aft, begging to get a drink. He had been wounded severely in the right arm with a piece of langridge shot, and the left was so bruised that he could not lift the jug to his head. De Squaw [a German member of the Genoa's crew], who had been working the gun with an activity and smartness that surprised me for a man of his age, took the jug, and after skimming back the blood and dirt from the top of the cask, filled it, and offered it to the officer; but just as he was in the act of holding it to the wounded man's mouth, he dropped a mangled corpse, being nearly cut in pieces with grape-shot.... Cool, however, as a British sailor is in danger, nothing can approach the Turk in this respect. George Finney had hauled one into the boat [they had been taking a hawser across to Codrington's Asia to haul her clear of a fireship], a fine looking fellow, and elegantly dressed. He was no sooner seated in the bow of the boat, than taking out a portable apparatus, he began to fill his pipe, which having done, he struck a light from the same conveniency, and commenced sending forth with

inconceivable apathy, volumes of smoke from his mouth....
Another instance of Turkish coolness I may mention,
which, though it did not happen in our ship, was told
me under well-authenticated circumstances. Some of the
crew of the French frigate *Alcyone* had picked up a Turk,
who by his dress appeared to be a person of rank in their
navy. When he was brought aboard, he found his arm so
shattered that it would need to undergo amputation; so
he made his way down the cockpit ladder with as much
ease as if he had made a prize of the frigate. He pointed
to his shattered arm, and made signs to the surgeon that
he wanted it off. The surgeon obliged him so far, and
having bound up the stump and bandaged it properly, the
Turk made his way to the deck, and plunging into the
water, swam to his own vessel that was opposed along
with another to the very frigate he had been aboard of.
He was seen climbing the side with his one arm, but had
not been aboard many minutes, when it blew up....

The cockpit, situated under the lower deck, where the
surgeon and his mates attended to the wounded, presented
its usual dismal spectacle in the ships engaged at Navarino,
as in all other sea battles over the centuries:

The stifled groans, the figures of the surgeon and his
mates, their bare arms and faces smeared with blood, and
others screaming under the amputating knife, formed a
horrid scene of misery, and made a hideous contrast to
the 'pomp, pride and circumstances of glorious war'.

There was one great difference from the past. The Unknown
Sailor was now able to express himself, and tell future
generations of 'the way it was', for the first time in all the
centuries.

CHAPTER SEVEN

The Great Change

It was hardly surprising that it should be a new nation, the United States, that would be the first to adopt steam propulsion for its navy in the nineteenth century. Untouched by any great traditions of the past that would lay a deadening hand upon present and future, the United States was the natural home of the new world of iron-built vessels propelled by steam-driven screws, and the great gun with a rifled bore. It is interesting to reflect, however, that even before this revolution in sea power the United States had shown that it would also prove a formidable rival to any of the older nations in the building and fighting of the old type of sail-driven warships with traditional smooth-bore guns.

In the war of 1812-14 the British navy on several occasions received, a salutary shock, in single ship engagements between its frigates and those of the Americans. British sea officers had tended to become somewhat complacent by this date about the ability of their ships and their men to win such individual contests, so to find that their former colony was able to produce frigates that appeared to be stronger, faster and sounder than their own brought home to them that in sea warfare there is no respite from eternal vigilance. The seed of this imposing new United States navy may be traced to correspondence between American designer Joshua Humphreys and the Minister of Finance, Robert Morris, in which he wrote:

From the present appearance of affairs I believe it is time

this country was possessed of a navy; but as that is yet to be raised, I have ventured a few remarks on the subject.

Ships that compose the European navies are generally distinguished by their rates; but as the situation and depth of water of our coasts and harbours are different in some degrees from those in Europe, and as our navy for a considerable time will be inferior in numbers, we are to consider what size ships will be most formidable, and be an over-match for those of an enemy; such frigates as in blowing weather would be an overmatch for double-deck ships, and in light winds to evade coming to action; or double-deck ships that would be an overmatch for common double-deck ships, and in blowing weather superior to ships of three decks, or in calm weather or light winds to outsail them. Ships built on these principles will render those of an enemy in a degree useless, or require a greater number before they dare attack our ships.... As such ships will cost a large sum of money, they should be built of the best materials that could possibly be procured....

America of course had to hand a scarcely touched continent for all such materials, at a time when Britain, for instance, had savagely depleted its native timbers and was very dependent on the Baltic countries for oak and many other materials. To secure respect for her neutral flag from both Britain and France, Congress appropriated funds for six frigates, one of which the USS *Constitution* later distinguished herself in engagements, similar to those which her designer Humphreys had envisaged, against the British in the war of 1812-14. (Known affectionately by the American nation as 'Old Ironsides', she has been restored and rests in Boston Harbour, the subject of a veneration by streams of annual visitors akin to *Victory* in Portsmouth.

Although these American frigates were in no way 'great ships', they were built to a calibre not far different from that of a ship of the line; and with the American designers' knowledge of their own waters and coastlines had the speedy ability that Joshua Humphreys had envisaged. Nominally rated at forty four guns, they carried more than fifty — a combination of thirty 24-pounders on the gun deck and twenty-two 32-pound carronades on the upper deck. They also carried two long 24-pounders and a long 18-pounder on the upper deck. Following the British fashion, carronades had been introduced so that if it ever came to close-quarters work with a larger ship (naturally to be avoided), they could administer an unexpectedly heavy blow. As typical of her class, *Constitution*'s hull was formed of more than twenty inches of frames and planking and, in place of iron fastenings, she had reverted to an older but even stronger method — better, too, since she was coppered — being fastened with wooden treenails. Two hundred and four feet overall she was 175 on her waterline, with a beam of 43½ feet, and a maximum draft of 23 feet. Her tonnage was about 1500 and in common with all other American warships of her time she set a very high rig indeed: sky sails on all three masts, and staysails as follows: (between mizzen topmast and mainmast from above) mizzen top sky sail, staysail, mizzen royal staysail, mizzen topgallant skysail, mizzen topsail staysail; (between mainmast and foremast from above) main skysail staysail, main royal staysail, upper and lower main topgallant staysails, main topgallant mast staysail, main topmast staysail. On the jib boom going forwards she carried: fore-topmast staysail, jib, flying jib, and outer flying jib. The sailorizing work involved with this spread of canvas (over 42,000 square feet) is awe inspiring. All sails, incidentally, were of flax and they required over two miles of hemp cordage for the running rigging. Records show that her top speed was about 13½ knots — little wonder that she could outsail (and indeed outfight) any British or French ships rated of the same class. She was bigger, more powerful, and faster.

Somewhat late in the day, but wisely mistrustful of the European powers, America decided that she too would need some great ships — more to serve as a warning to potential aggressors than for any real purpose along her coastline.

In these the Americans were not so successful, having no traditions of great ship building even though they had the craftsmen and all the materials for a large fleet of ships of the line. Her answer to the European 74s was a ship like *Franklin,* with a total number of 82 guns, including carronades. All her main armament consisted of 32-pounders, short ones on the upper deck and long ones on the gun deck. Coming from a large continent and with an immense wealth of reserves behind them the Americans, then as now, tended to 'think big' — not always successfully. In their smaller ships, like *Constitution,* their designers and craftsmen foreshadowed their country's fast schooners and the immensely successful later American 'clippers' that would be almost unrivalled in passage making and cargo carrying. Some of their ships of the line turned out to be unable to mount the number of guns planned, or handled badly and proved expensive to run. The largest of these, *Pennsylvania,* had a keel length of 195 feet, and was rated as a 120-gun ship but could actually mount more than this, making her at the time the greatest ship in the world. (Seen in a picture at the National Maritime Museum, it is clear that she mounted guns not on three decks alone, but even on the fourth known as the 'spar deck' made by uniting the forecastle and quarterdeck.) Never tested in any action, *Pennsylvania,* like *Ohio* and others, were enough to show Europe what America could do. But by the time this had been noted by other powers, the great age of sail — at least as regards warships — had given way to steam.

The British Admiralty began to use steam tugs for harbour use not long after the end of the Napoleonic wars. It is untrue that their lordships, as has sometimes been implied, were totally averse to the whole conception of coal, steam and dirty engines being involved in their navy. What they could not see at this phase in the development of the steam engine was how it could possibly apply to warships: engines took up a lot of space in the hull (which was needed for men and guns); coal consumption was high and precluded any use except for short distance work;

and, furthermore, paddle wheels were absurdly vulnerable since a single round shot would smash them. All this was indeed true, and it was not until the invention of the screw propellor that the steam warship became worthy of consideration. The screw itself was nothing new, being as old as Archimedes, but its practical application to fighting vessels — particularly since those of Britain required long-range fuel supply to maintain her sea lanes — had yet to be proved. Furthermore, so long as the gunpower of the great warship depended upon rows of smooth-bore guns ranged in banks in its sides the problems of coal consumption and space for both fuel and engines remained. In the country where the Industrial Revolution had begun, it was unlikely that the authorities were unaware of the future potential of the steam engine (however reluctant men brought up in sail might be to consider it), but the whole concept had first of all to be forced upon them for the good reason that Bernard Brodie has given *(Sea Power in the Machine Age)*: 'It was an old maxim in the British Admiralty that Great Britain ought never to initiate any naval innovation destined to render existing material obsolete, but that she should be prepared to outstrip any other power initiating such a change.' During the nineteenth century any number of such innovations would occur and require outstripping. In fact, it could be said that the whole century in all countries was spent in trying to adapt everything, including ships, to all the changes brought about by the new machine age.

One man, John Ericsson, was to have more effect on the future evolution of naval ships than almost any other, many as were the claimants to the development of the screw propeller and other developments in warships. In 1836, having left the Swedish army, where his engineering brilliance had already been remarked, he had come to England and taken out his patent of a screw propeller. He had offered it first to the Admiralty who, despite a successful demonstration of its potentials, were not sufficiently impressed for reasons that have been given above but, although the priority of his invention could not be maintained, he was later awarded a one-fifth share of the £20,000 given by the Admiralty for it. No doubt the manufacturers of paddle-wheels and the engines suitable for them, together with their engineers, brought natural pressure to bear against the adoption of the propeller, but it was not until Ericsson and others had worked out plans for engines that could be sited entirely below the waterline as well as boiler systems with greater pressures and lower fuel consumptions that the great changeover became practicable. At this same time, a Captain Stockton of the young US Navy was in London and gave Ericsson an order for a small iron vessel to be built at Birkenhead and fitted with Ericsson's engines and a screw. The vessel reached New York in 1839 and was followed a few months later by the inventor. He was to become an American citizen and reside there for the rest of his life, devoting to this new receptive country his immense mechanical talents. These were quickly recognized, and in 1843 the first screw warship, the USS *Princeton* was launched, a 10-gun sloop with a six-bladed screw of Ericsson's design and driven by engines that gave her about 13 knots.

Ericsson's later work on defensive armour for ships and his early plans for an armoured steam-driven vessel, lying low in the water, were even more eclipsed by his work on the armoured circular turret mounted on a turntable and carrying heavy guns. It was to revolutionize naval warfare and speed on its way to extinction the great sailing warships. Once guns could be centrally mounted, all the old conceptions of naval warfare and the siting of great batteries in the sides themselves were overthrown. This was in the future, however, and in the meantime from France came the invention that was to effect a further radical change in a world which basically had remained in a state of stasis since the time of Henry VIII.

For all those years, guns of every navy had fired solid shot and in recent years mostly from 32-pounder guns. There also existed case or grape shot for close quarters work, fired mainly by light guns and consisting of small shot contained in cylinders or bags held together between two circular iron plates linked by a spindle. The latter were antipersonnel in the main and were indeed as old as Henry VIII's navy, some light guns already loaded with powder and hailshot for use against the invading French having been recovered intact from *Mary Rose*.

Suddenly in 1837 the French began to arm their navy with guns that fired hollow shells filled with gunpowder. The hollow shell was nothing new in itself in military warfare, having been used in the shape of hand grenades for several centuries, while as early as the sixteenth century clay pots filled with inflammable substances known as Greek Fire had been used from castle and fortress walls, ignited with a fuse and dropped on attackers. Later had come the cast-iron grenade, and first of all at sea the bomb fired from a wide-mouthed mortar. Bomb vessels had been designed to carry these but they clearly had limited scope for their use, although the mortar and the bomb were efficient. They were safe to use since the fuse of the bomb projected outside the muzzle and, if it had been lit and there was any delay in firing the gun, the fuse could be quickly cut. The problem of how to use something similar in long guns like 32-pounders had long taxed the experts, for the advantage of being able to hurl an explosive shell against wooden-built warships was obviously apparent, fire being at all time their greatest hazard.

Colonel Paixhans, a French army officer, had suggested in a technical publication *La Nouvelle Force Maritime* that instead of the old mortars firing bombs in a high trajectory, direct-aim guns firing explosive shells in a flat trajectory should be developed for sea warfare, and had gone ahead to test one out at Brest in 1824. The problem of how to ignite the shell, once down the bore of a long gun, was solved by the fact that as the projectiles of cast-iron shot were never exactly spherical there was always some amount of windage between it and the bore. The new shell shot could therefore be loaded into a gun and rest there as safely as if it was solid shot until the gun was actually fired — then the flames of the explosion as they expelled the shell also ignited its fuse. A broadside, or even only a few of such shells, hitting another warship would instantly turn it into an inextinguishable sea of flames.

Not for the last time the French had made a breakthrough in naval affairs that left all other navies virtually obsolete. It was fortunate for the British that no such discovery had been made in the Napoleonic wars for, even after themselves constructing similar type shells and guns, it would take years to effect the changeover on a large fleet. Eventually Woolwich armoury did produce an equivalent to the Paixhans' guns and shells and by the time that the Crimean War broke out British and French navies, allies on this occasion, were mostly equipped with shell guns.

Nevertheless the lesson was not fully learned by naval authorities, and particularly admirals, still insistent on great sailing warships, until the Russians declared their hand. Little considered previously any more than the Americans by British and French, the Russians sprang a surprise on 30 November 1853 when Admiral Nakhimov in command of six ships of the line, armed with 68-pounders firing explosive shells, attacked a Turkish squadron of frigates and corvettes lying at anchor in the roadstead of Sinope on the south coast of the Black Sea. Within minutes the Turkish ships were in flames — the first time in naval warfare that high-explosive shells had ever been used — and within minutes, as it were, a whole world came crashing down. The advocates of 'sail and wooden walls' could not ignore this portent, and even the builders of the new ironclad ships, constructed as they then were of iron plates fastened to wooden hulls, began to realize that ultimately it would have to be the all-iron hull. (The 'sacred' wooden decks were to remain for long to come.)

A year later, during the bombardment of Sevastopol it was the turn of British and French warships to come under the new shellfire, serious damage being inflicted on both allies, the British ship of the line HMS *Queen* being hit by three grenades in almost as many minutes, her guns' crews even abandoning their stations in the unexpected havoc that was caused. This was effectively the end of 'the old navy' — even though examples would continue to sail the seas for years to come. In the type of warfare then prevailing — ships against forts — it was clear that the only answer was to build the equivalent of floating, mobile fortresses: there was no time to build, let alone evolve, the great iron-clad, heavily-engined battleship of the future. The French, again quicker than the British (who had placed an order for something similar), were the first to produce three armoured gunboats which were in time to take part in the bombardment of the sea fortress of Kinburn in October 1855. Although hit many times themselves, the gunboats' armour stood up to the explosive shells fired against them while they, using similar types of shells, were able to silence the batteries ashore. *Dévastation, Lave* and *Tonnante,* however, were not even prototypes of the battleships of the future, being (as they had been designed to be) shallow-draft, suitable only for coastal waters, and having a maximum speed of 4 knots.

The whole of the latter part of the nineteenth century, as far as navy offices and architects were concerned, was really a search for its replacement. The ship of the future remained elusive. It was subject to so many constantly altering techniques and technologies and materials even, that it could be said that it remained permanently elusive. Certainly it would never be possible again to say, 'Now we have gone as far as we can go. Now we have produced the new model of "the great ship" that will dominate the oceans without challenge for generations.' In the years prior to World War I, it was felt perhaps that now the great battleship had reached its ultimate stage. As so often has proved the case since the industrial revolution changed man's world, nothing again would ever achieve a comfortable *status quo* — never again would there be centuries of the great sailing warship or millenia of the galley.

Although in the Crimean War, both in the Baltic and the Black Sea, there were still almost as many wooden ships of the line as there were combined sail and steamships, the lessons of that war were quickly drawn — wooden ships were death traps against shells. The British Board of Admiralty, however, continued to build a few wooden battleships and they could continue in use in distant parts of the globe. This innate conservatism towards which all service organizations of all countries are always prone — especially those with long traditions — would only yield to the threat of a foreign, and possibly hostile, power making some sudden advance. France was usually hostile, or had been through most of the centuries, and the British were shaken into action when, in the late 1850s, it was known that the French were going ahead with an ironclad fleet and that, like the British, they were already trying experiments with cast-iron rifled guns. Under Napoleon III's brilliant designer and Director-General of Construction, Dupuy de Lome, the French navy were building iron-clad armoured ships, to be fitted with rifled guns. That these first iron-clads in France were muzzle loaders, whereas in Britain Armstrong and Whitworth (still rivals at that time) had successfully produced rifled, breech-loading guns with a range of some five miles, did not lessen the concern. The first ship of the new class was, in fact, a conversion of a ninety-gun wooden warship, screw and steam-driven and appearing in her new guise as a 60-gun frigate. Famous because she was the first of her type, *La Gloire* had her wooden sides along the waterline and upwards protected by 5-inch armour plating. With a tonnage of over 5500, she was propelled at a speed of 13 knots by engines developing 4200 hp. The immediate British reaction, according to that unspoken rule, was to build a larger and more heavily-gunned ship, while the French were following *La Gloire* with a class of armoured ships built throughout of iron. All these were three-masted with a mixed squaresail and fore- and aft-rig, though by now it was becoming evident that it was the sails that were auxiliary, and not the engines. Originally armed with the French rifled muzzle loaders, they were changed to breechloaders in due course. (It is a curious fact that the cannon of the first great ships should some of them have been breech loaders, only to have been discarded for muzzle loaders for centuries.)

Warrior was the first British iron clad, to be swiftly followed by her sister-ship *Black Prince*. With a displacement of over 9000 tons, she was in her time the greatest warship in the world, causing the Emperor Louis Napoleon to remark wryly that compared with all others she 'looked like a black snake among the rabbits'.

Snakelike she was, in that she was 380 feet overall; this great length being necessitated by the fact that, when she was built, the Admiralty had not made up their minds about the Armstrong breech loaders, and she had to accommodate a single gun deck with ports for forty 68-pounder muzzle loaders. Rare in this confusing age of change, when grace seemed to have departed from great ships, she was remarkable for her lines — not so unlike contemporary clippers except for her greater length — with schooner bows and frigate stern. She was three-masted and square-rigged and under power had attained a speed of over fourteen knots. There were two great drawbacks to this graceful great ship, the first being that her 4½ inch wrought-iron armour belts, while protecting her engines and her guns, did not extend all the way fore and aft, thus leaving bows and stern unprotected. The other drawback to both *Warrior* and *Black Prince* (and a fatal one it could have been if ever brought to action) was that their great length made them difficult to handle at sea whether under sail or under power. The French, while concerned about these new ships of their old enemy, were probably right in maintaining that the *Gloire* class, although smaller and slightly slower, were with their continuous armoured belt and their great manoeuvrability more efficient warships. In any case, the test never came and one of the reasons for the *Pax Britannica* upon the high seas, that prevailed right up to World War I, was that the British kept constantly one ahead of all their rivals in naval ship building — most reluctantly though they did so. Often forgotten in the late twentieth century, particularly perhaps by the former beneficiaries of it, is that almost a century of peace, maintained very largely by British great ships, enabled colonies and former colonies to grow and develop without having to look nervously towards their coastlines, or spend enormous sums on the development of their own navies.

Interestingly enough, of all vessels of the transition period in warship design the only one that has survived in any country is *Warrior* herself. From her commissioning in 1861 until she was relegated to the reserves in 1875 she never fired a shot in anger, nor was there ever any need for her to do so, largely because ships like her had by their presence on the high seas ensured the preservation of peace. Her career, one might say, was distinguished by the very fact that it was in warlike terms undistinguished.... Staying afloat — a tribute to her wrought-iron hull — during all the succeeding years, through two world wars, in various lowly capacities, she ended apparently ignominiously (to the few who knew her origins) as Hulk C77 at Milford Haven in Wales. As a floating jetty for oil tankers, with a helicopter pad and 250 tons of concrete on her deck, *Warrior* had to all intents and purposes disappeared, along with hundreds of other great ships that had been built in the century. However, the modern interest in naval and industrial archaeology has led to this veteran of the nineteenth century being restored. Ultimately, when the lengthy and extremely expensive operation is completed, it is hoped that she will join other more famous veterans like *Mary Rose* and *Victory* in a naval heritage centre at Portsmouth.

To follow the erratic course of naval warship design in the nineteenth century would be to wander down many byways. For a very brief time *Warrior* held sway, but in the ever-changing technology of the nineteenth century, such ships — like modern fighter aircraft and other weapons — were obsolescent almost as soon as they were launched. Since no wars occurred to prove them one against the other, they disappeared from sight.

One duel, which has been written about as much as any of the great naval actions of the past, was the fight between the Confederate armour-clad ship *Virginia* (ex-steam frigate *Merrimack)* and the Union armour-clad, turret-ship, *Monitor.* The interest that this engagement aroused not only in America but throughout the world, where it continued to form the subject of argument among naval designers for some time to come, was due to a number of factors. For the non-American general audience its interest lay in the fact that it was a spectacular incident in the war between the divided American states, the outcome of which concerned both politicians and businessmen alike; for the navies of the world it focussed on the contest between a turret ship and a casemate ship; and for all onlookers in a period of peace it was the first engagement between these ugly, suspicious looking vessels driven by steam that seemed to have taken over from the long recognized and handsome-looking warships of the past. The decorative beauty of the old great ship would never be recaptured, that was recognized. In the future, sheer grandeur and powerful dignity in steel and giant guns would come to represent that quality, but it must be said that in the age of transition, almost inevitably, warships were ugly.

When the Union troops had withdrawn from Norfolk, Virginia, in 1861, on the secession of that State, they lost their finest navy yard and were forced to scuttle a number of ships that were lying there. Among them was the powerful wooden, steam frigate *Merrimack*, whose engines were under repair at the time. The Confederates, who were without a navy, raised her, cut away such of the gun deck as was burnt, and fitted her with a casemate of oak beams whose sloping sides they armoured to a depth of four inches, with rolled railway iron — that being the best that they had available. The ends of the casemate were radiused and in the centre, apart from the funnel, there protruded only a small wheelhouse with inclined walls, similarly armoured. She was also fitted with a primitive ram, for a curiosity about this and others of the new warships that were to follow her was that the ram of the galley made a comeback that would, indeed, last right up to World War I. (Whereas ramming the enemy had been an impossibility under sail, steam propulsion like oar propulsion provided the impetus.) *Virginia,* as she was renamed, was armed with six 9-inch guns, two 6.4-inch rifled guns, and two 7-inch guns, and with her one engine could make about 9 knots.

Meanwhile the Union, concerned about their almost impossible blockade of 3000 miles of coastline, particularly Hampton Roads, the estuary of the James river and the waterways to Richmond, was even more concerned when the report reached them of the Confederates putting together a navy, in particular a large ironclad. A design by John Ericsson, for a most unusual turret ship, which had long ago been offered to Napoleon III and turned down, had for years lain filed in the inventor's workshop; it was hauled out and refurbished and submitted to the Navy Department. It was so unlike anything ever before conceived as a warship that immense scepticism was aroused (the inventor himself had called it 'aquatic device').

The armour-clad *Virginia (Merrimack)* had meanwhile appeared unexpectedly off Hampton Roads and taken by surprise the squadron stationed there, blockading the James River. She opened fire first on the 24-gun *Cumberland,* the latter replying with her broadsides. Even as the range closed, *Virginia* continuing to fire her two forward 7-inch, *Cumberland* found that her shot was merely bouncing or dropping from *Virginia's* sides quite ineffectually. Finally, the Confederate ironclad administered the *coup de grace* by ramming her. She left her ram behind her in *Cumberland* as she backed away, while the latter heeled over and sank with heavy loss of life. The frigate *Congress* had by now got sail on her and come into action, only to find she was equally powerless against those armoured sides. Running aground in the shallows, *Congress* lay like an object for target practice by *Virginia* for over an hour, until she was left a burning wreck with many casualties. Two other ships of the squadron, which tugs were endeavouring to tow to safety from this seemingly-impregnable monster, ran aground, while *Virginia* steamed away to effect repairs to her bows necessitated by the tearing away of the ram. In the successful action against the two Union ships, although hit constantly, she had lost only ten men dead or wounded and had two guns disabled. She confidently expected to return next day and finish off anything that was left of the blockading squadron.

The following morning, coming back for the further kill, *Virginia* was as disconcerted as the vessels in Hampton Roads had been by her the day before, when *Monitor,* which by sheer coincidence had arrived the previous night, made her appearance. This strange, low silhouette creeping out against her must have proved more than alarming to any who first observed it. They were certainly an unconventional pair: the one with an armoured casemate on a conventional basic hull (without masts or rigging), and the other appearing to be little more than an armoured turret with two large guns, the water breaking across its decks out of which, forward of the turret, the pilot-box protruded.

The action between them went on almost continuously for four hours, neither ship being able to deliver a death blow to the other. *Monitor* had a slow rate of fire and was using too weak a propellant charge of powder, while *Virginia* found that, apart from finding the other's turret a small and difficult target, she was unable to damage its armour. Most of the contest was fought at close quarters, but neither ship was able to do any effective damage to the other and it ended inconclusively. *Virginia* was the only one to suffer any real damage — her funnel gone, some of her armour started, and two gun ports out of action, while the commander of *Monitor* was injured by a direct hit on the pilot house. No one was killed on either side, despite each receiving many hits. President Lincoln, however, sensed immediately the potential of *Monitor,* and many more of these armour-clad, Ericsson-invented vessels were at once ordered. Worldwide, they would give a name to a whole new type of vessels, 'monitors'.

International naval opinion was as indecisive as this curious contest had been — and was to remain so. In navy offices and design staffs the argument would continue as to the advantages of the turret or the ram, or a combination of both. The fact that *Monitor* had been able successfully to avoid several attempts by *Virginia* to ram her (due simply to her greater manoeuvrability) was ignored by those in favour of the ram, while the turret supporters pointed to the damage inflicted on the Confederate vessel by large guns in a centre-line turret. One thing was noticeable: there was no argument against armour plating, and the voices of old admirals in defence of sail were forever silenced.

CHAPTER EIGHT

The Age of Experiment

The general conclusion drawn from the American Civil War was that vessels like *Monitor* — except for their turrets — were little more than adaptations or improvements on the earlier French floating forts such as *Dévastation*. Along the American east coast, and particularly in the estuary area for which the first of this class had been specifically designed, they might serve their purpose. Like their French predecessors at Kinburn, they were certainly not sea-going warships. They would not be viable in the English Channel, let alone on the great sea routes of the world over which the Royal Navy had to keep watch and ward. As if to confirm this view, the prototype *Monitor* sank in a gale off Cape Hatteras less than a year after she had been launched. The *Virginia (Merrimack)* type of casemate ship had also disclosed its weaknesses, for it was clear that even if she had been more powerfully engined such a vessel was no more than a compromise (which was true) between the old sailing warship and the floating battery. Again, they were not suitable for the high seas nor for the kind of fleet action that had to be expected if ever there were another war between any of the major powers.

Unhampered by previous conventions and with their New World, outward-looking natures, the Americans were prepared to 'try anything once', and even more than once. Some of their experiments, while perhaps causing unease in European circles, did not seem as if they would ever be relevant to the world that thought in terms of great fleets and fleet engagements. Submarines, for instance, which were ultimately to change the whole face of sea warfare, and which already had quite a long history (rather like aircraft before any were effective), were first seriously used in the American Civil War. The first warship in history sunk by a 'submersible' (rather than a true submarine) was the Union's *Housatonic* on blockade duties off Charleston, where the Confederate craft blew her up by a torpedo fixed on the end of a spar attached to the bows of the boat. The 'submersible' herself was later swamped through an open hatch and sank, together with her crew of nine men. But such minor epics in American history were somewhat ignored by Europeans, concentrating more on the main developments which they could see taking place in this — to them remote — test bed of new fighting ships. (France again was to be the first in Europe with a true submarine, powered underwater by an electric motor, and launched in 1888.)

Other American single turret ships followed after *Monitor* — only the pilot house was now sensibly sited on top of the turret, the whole being covered with eleven inches of armour plate and armed with two guns, one 11-inch and the other 15-inch, both smooth-bore Dahlgren guns. Being shallow draught like the prototype, they also were found dangerous in a seaway and led to Ericsson designing larger versions with a draught of over twenty feet. The first of these still only mounted one turret but later versions had two, linked by a flying bridge. Despite their draught, these were also designed to have their decks only a few feet above water level — so as to display a minimum target — while their draught was to accommodate engines designed to take them at sixteen knots, as well as giving them a long range coal supply. They never reached their designed speed because of their underwater displacement, as well as the fact that when underway in anything other than a flat calm their upper decks were awash, the whole design presenting considerable water resistance. They were seagoing, however, one crossing the Atlantic and another rounding Cape Horn.

The main effect of the ships that evolved during the American Civil War was to direct the attention of European navies to the armoured turret and the ram. The centre-line turret was to stand the test of time and survive well into the twentieth century, when the battleship with great guns became obsolete (her fire power overwhelmed by the strike capability of aircraft loaded with bombs or torpedoes and launched from what had become the new great ship, the aircraft carrier). It was *Monitor,* naturally, that had drawn attention to the turret, but it was *Virginia (Merrimack)* whose initial success with the ram at Hampton Roads (leading to other Confederate vessels being built on the same basic lines) had given an unmerited prestige to the ram. What was often ignored by the onlookers from afar, and in days of still comparatively primitive communications, was that these early engagements, and others that would follow in the Civil War, had almost without exception taken place not only in coastal waters but in shallow waters at that. Something else that had not been tested was the ability of any such ships to operate in large battle fleets together, which would clearly be necessary in any conflict between European powers.

Disturbed by the evidence of all these changes and determined as ever to keep a step ahead of any foreign power, the British Admiralty was also pressured by a general clamour in the press to achieve an up-to-date navy that possessed turreted ironclads. Captain Coles, RN, one of the most vociferous of these advocates of the new, was now entrusted with the job of converting the 120-gun *Royal Sovereign* into the first British turret ship. Her hull was cut down to her lower gun deck and she was given four turrets, designed for use as an ironclad for coastal defence. She was an experiment but no more, and since Coles had by now supervised the construction of an iron hulled ship, *Prince Albert,* the latter may be considered the first real British turreted ironclad. Displacing 4000 tons, *Prince Albert* had an armament of four 9-inch guns, mounted in four separate turrets on the upper deck. But both of these vessels could only be considered of use for coastal defence since, on account of their heavy-weight turrets, they necessarily had to have small freeboards in order to maintain stability. Britain was looking ultimately for ocean-going great ships, and it was clear that neither of these two first models passed the test. A new chief constructor of the Royal Navy was to favour the central battery ship, following the French *Magenta,* but this meant a reduction in the number of guns and it was the casemate ship that was the first to be adopted by Britain and most navies, despite the fact that an ironclad turreted ship designed by Coles had enabled the Danes to gain a success at sea during a dispute with Prussia.

The first battle between ironclad fleets was naturally watched by all nations with the greatest interest, for up to now whether with turrets or casemates, they had only met in individual encounters. Many old admirals and others had naturally continued to maintain that, when it came to a fleet action, it would soon be seen that only 'real' ships could be handled properly and achieve a conclusive success in the old mode. In June 1886 a major sea battle was fought in the Mediterranean between Italy and Austria, a battle which was won, despite the odds, by the smaller and older fleet, and from the results of which the other European powers were to draw the wrong conclusions. The lesson they failed to learn was that as much importance still lay with the training of crews, their morale, and of course the morale of their officers. It was here that the Austrians prevailed over the Italians.

Italy had gone to war with Austria in June 1886, having what certainly appeared to be by far the superior navy. For a start, she had the brand new *Affondatore*. She was of 4000 tons, iron-built, heavily-armoured, with two 10-inch, rifled 300-pounder Armstrong guns, and designed with a heavy spurbow for ramming. Italy also had eleven other armoured ships, four of them all of iron. While both fleets were principally armed with Armstrong guns, nearly all those of the Italians were rifled, and fired a far greater weight of metal than the Austrians. Austria had only seven ironclads, all built of wood, heavily armoured; the two largest of 5000 tons mounting eighteen smooth bore 48-pounders.

The Austrian crews, however, had been highly trained and exercised in fleet operations and ramming tactics since May, while the Italian crews were badly trained and suffering from that disease which Nelson had long ago diagnosed: 'Lying in harbour, which rots ships and rots men.' The salient difference, however, lay in the character of the admirals: Count Persano, the Italian, and von Tegethoff, the Austrian.

Admiral Persano seems to have been very much the product of the comfortable nineteenth century, an admiral who had never expected to fight a battle, and who seems to have had no conception of strategy or of tactics. He placed great faith in his new ship, *Affondatore* (still on passage from Britain when war broke out), and he resolutely refused to engage the Austrians in any way until she had joined him. Von Tegethoff, on the other hand, had had as active a service afloat as was possible in those days, a commander during the Crimean War and again as a commander in action against the Danes in 1864. In June 1886 he set out from the Austrian base of Pola in the Adriatic with six ironclads, five gunboats, a wooden frigate and a scouting steamer, and steamed south to Ancona where Admiral Persano was lying with eleven ironclads (still lacking *Affondatore*) and a number of other vessels. Having chased an Italian despatch vessel into the port, Tegethoff cleared for action and steamed up and down, as if challenging Persano to come out and fight. The latter was not moving without his eagerly awaited ship, later excusing himself to his government on the grounds that his ships had not yet completed their fitting out. This preliminary episode left Austrian morale very high and the Italian equally depressed. A further foray by his fleet and continued exercises at sea made Tegethoff's men and officers skilful in manoeuvres and highly trained. He knew that, if the two fleets ever engaged, he would be facing more ships and more modern ships as well as a great superiority in gun power. He could only combat this by having an organized pattern of aggressive tactics and a perfectly tuned instrument to hand. The war on land was going badly for Italy, the Austrians had won a battle at Custozza in the north, and the Italian government was determined that the navy should redeem the situation by a victory at sea. (They were looking for a bargaining counter in the event of a truce.) Count Persano, who had finally been joined by *Affondatore* and so had no further excuse for delay, was literally forced to take some action under threat of losing his command — and he took the worst action possible.

His course was clear: he had a preponderance of better-armed ships, his opponent was for the moment back in Pola, and he should have set about the blockade of that port, ready to fight Tegethoff if he came out. Instead he proposed that he should descend with a small armed force on the fortified Dalmatian island of Lissa, with his fleet bombarding the Austrian gun positions prior to landing troops. On 19 July the bombardment of Lissa began, the soldiers waiting anxiously in a squadron of wooden ships accompanied by gunboats. It was expected that the forts would be sufficiently reduced over the following day for a landing to be made on the morning of the 20th. Persano now discovered that shore fortresses (and these were old and not heavily gunned) are difficult targets to subdue, while the bombarding vessels themselves are conspicuous targets on the open face of the sea. One of the Italian ironclads, *Formidabile,* was heavily hit, suffering many casualties, and had to be sent back to Ancona while, on the morning of the 20th, another had to be detailed off to give protection to the wooden ships during the proposed landing operations. These were never to take place for, on hearing of the attack on Lissa, Tegethoff had immediately ordered the Austrian fleet to sea. He had left with every available ship, ironclads and unarmoured wooden ships alike, formed in three V-shaped divisions. Ahead of them went a fast armed liner to act as scout, followed by the seven ironclads, with Tegethoff at the head of the V in his flagship *Ferdinand Max*. Behind these came the second wave of unarmoured wooden ships in similar formation, and lastly the third division, formed of small gunboats. Tegethoff intended in Nelson-style, to provoke a mêlée, relying on the better training of his crews and their high morale against the greater firepower of the other side. Steaming hard through the night — a tribute to their training that they managed to keep formation — Tegethoff hoped to attack the Italians as early as possible on the following day.

Next morning an Italian scouting vessel reported the approach of the Austrians and Persano countermanded the orders for landing troops (men were already in the boats), and broke off the bombardment of the forts. He had not expected so swift a reaction by the Austrians. Possibly he had hoped that he could get away with reducing the defences of Lissa, land his troops, and see the Italian flag hauled up over the island, before returning safely to Ancona.... He seems to have had no battle plan prepared in the very likely event that the Austrians would put to sea the moment they had news of the Italian attack. As the smoke of the enemy advancing over the horizon became visible, he formed his ten ironclads into line ahead and steered across the enemy's lines of advance to protect his invasion convoy. At this crucial moment he made his greatest mistake of all. He had been flying his flag in the wooden ironclad *Re d'Italia,* lying fourth in the line ahead of the new *Affondatore.* He now decided to change his flag to *Affondatore* — the rest of his fleet, being ignorant of this, still looked to the *Re d'Italia* for orders. Persano had lost control from this moment onwards. The operation made it necessary for *Re d'Italia* and the ships astern of her to reduce speed, with the result that a gap opened in the Italian line as the leading ships drew away. Persano had thus created the very situation which attacking commanders over past centuries had had to work long and arduously to achieve.

Tegethoff, on sighting the enemy, had hoisted the signal to his advancing formation of ironclads to 'Ram and sink the enemy' — not because they were specially designed to ram (indeed they had only blunt rams) but because he saw this as the best way of overcoming the superior fire power of the Italians. The latter, meanwhile, opened a rapid but ill-directed fire at 1000 yards; the Austrians not replying until the range was down to about 300 yards. Tegethoff directed his ironclads straight for the gap in the Italian line and burst through, four of his ships then turning to port to engage the Italian van, and the other three to starboard to engage the enemy's centre. Meanwhile the Austrian second division of wooden ships led by *Kaiser* also followed through, and carried on to engage the Italian rear. In the mêlée that developed, where in theory the weight of the Italian guns should have been devastating, it was the trained and disciplined coolness of the Austrians that prevailed. The Italian ironclad *Re di Portogallo* was rammed by the old *Kaiser*, the latter being badly damaged in the encounter while the Italian ironclad suffered comparatively little harm. *Kaiser* then proceeded to take cover under the protection of the shore forts, while in the centre the battle raged around *Re d'Italia*, which the Austrians still presumed to be Persano's flagship. Tegethoff in *Ferdinand Max* had succeeded in ramming both her and the ironclad *Palestro*, but had only managed to strike them glancing blows.

One thing to emerge from the action (passing unnoticed by world opinion at the time) was that it was very difficult to ram a steam-propelled vessel in view of its evasive powers. The *Affondatore*, for instance, had been designed as a ram ship, and yet, although Persano made repeated attempts to ram the enemy, all were avoided. In the fog of smoke that so many coal-fired vessels made within a constricted area on a still day, uncertainty prevailed as to the position of individual ships at any given moment. Indeed, the only successful ramming action of the day occurred when the captain of Tegethoff's *Ferdinand Max* himself clambered up the mizzen rigging. He shouted down that he could see *Re d'Italia* lying stopped and indicated where she lay. (She had been hit by a shell which had temporarily caused her to come to a halt.) Before she could get under way again, Tegethoff's flagship charged out of the smoke at full speed and rammed her amidships. A vast hole was torn in her side and, as *Ferdinand Max* reversed her engines and drew away, *Re d'Italia* heeled over and instantly sank, taking hundreds down with her. During the battle, which lasted several hours, the Italian ironclad *Palestro* (which suffered from the same design defect as the never tested British *Warrior)* was hit by a shell in her unarmoured stern. She caught fire and had to retire from the action. Later on, after the battle was over and both sides were withdrawing, the fire became unmanageable and she blew up.

Tegethoff, having succeeded in breaking through the Italian line and having by sheer aggressive tactics also succeeded in the confused battle that followed, now formed his ironclads in line and proceeded to follow his wooden ships under the protective guns of Lissa. Persano himself withdrew his fleet into the channel between Lissa and another smaller island, and was fully expected by the Austrians to renew the battle on the following day. They had achieved their main aim in any case — that of breaking between the investing enemy and Lissa. They lay at anchor in the island's port repairing their damage overnight, and prepared to resume action as soon as necessary. But by the 22nd it was seen that the Italians had disappeared, having withdrawn to Ancona — where Persano was foolish enough to announce a great victory. The truth became apparent only too soon, and the added disaster of the admiral's new *Affondatore,* damaged by unrecorded shell hits in the battle, sinking at her moorings during an onshore blow, completed his ruin. He was court-martialled and dismissed the navy, while the Austrian Tegethoff deservedly became the hero of his country. He was lucky to a great extent for, while certainly proving that aggression pays in warfare, he had met with a vacillating admiral (if no more), and the success which clinched the battle — the sinking of *Re d'Italia* — should never have been allowed to happen. Properly handled by trained officers and gunners, Persano's *Affondatore* alone should have been capable of crippling or sinking the leading Austrian ironclads at long range, thus preventing the occurrence of such an old-fashioned mêlée as Tegethoff had managed to secure.

The wrong conclusions, as has been said, were drawn by

other nations from the battle of Lissa. One thing certainly had been clearly demonstrated — that an unarmoured ship (there were still its advocates) was a thing of the past. But the sinking of *Re d'Italia* by ramming made an unwarranted impression on world opinion, and from now on almost all navies designed their great ships with rams, and bows specially strengthened for this purpose. A careful study of the battle of Lissa should have shown how many attempts to ram had been successfully evaded or had been ineffectual — as in Tegethoff's first attack on *Re d'Italia* and *Palestro* — while his second successful attack had been due to the unusual circumstances that the Italian ship had no way upon her at the time. The future increase in the power and range of guns was soon to mean that there would be few opportunities again for close quarters action — something that was considerably reinforced by the advent of the Whitehead torpedo, a deadly weapon which was adopted by almost all navies in the 1870s.

The absence of any fleet actions in the years after Lissa left the navies of the world to develop without any test bed, and indeed so many things were changing in technology that ship after ship (like *Warrior*) were obsolete within a year or two of their launch and enjoyed a long life without seeing any action. They provided mainly a means of 'showing the flag' in foreign ports, and, in the case of the colonial powers, of reassuring their colonists in distant lands that the mother country's protection was available, while deterring any potential dissidents from attempting to overthrow the regime. Such isolated incidents that did occur were relatively unimportant clashes between individual ships (in the Franco-Prussian War of 1870 and the Russo-Turkish war of 1878), revealing nothing to students of naval strategy and tactics nor to naval architects or constructors.

Occasionally out of the amorphous confusion of the nineteenth century drawings, documents and photographs of great ships there emerges one that immediately strikes the twentieth century viewer with something immediately recognizable as the ancestor of things to come. To Nathaniel

Barnaby, later Director of Naval Construction, must largely be ascribed the credit for the first battleship that is instantly recognizable as such to the modern eye, and the ship which was to become for all navies the prototype from which the new class developed. *Devastation*, laid down in 1869 and completed in 1873, was the first sea-going warship in which sails were completely dispensed with, and her appearance was naturally greeted with cries of horror. Yet she was to some extent the indirect product of the disaster that had befallen *Captain*, designed by Captain Coles, which had attempted to combine the traditional rig of the sea-going ship with steam and with two centre-line gun turrets. (The instability of the design had caused her to capsize and sink in a storm with all hands.) By removing the three masts, spars, rigging and sails, thus keeping down the topweight, Barnaby left *Devastation* with only a single pole mast in the centre, with a fighting top for machine guns. Her armament consisted of four 12-inch muzzle loaders in two turrets with armour plating of 10-14 inches, while the armour on the hull was 8½-12 inches thick. Two hundred and eighty five feet long by 62 feet wide, the *Devastation* was twin-screwed and had a range of 5000 miles. Provided that coaling depots were available (as they were in the widely distributed British Empire) ships like *Devastation* could no longer be faulted on the grounds that only sailing ships had sufficient range to cope with the demands of ocean warfare. She followed the ideas of her time in one thing, being equipped with a prominent ram, but as a precaution against being rammed herself she was subdivided into watertight compartments.

Although built only a decade later, *Devastation* would easily have been a match for a number of ships of the *Warrior* class. Yet she, in her turn, was to be outgunned almost immediately by the Italian *Duilio* and *Dandolo* mounting four 15-inch guns. They were larger than *Devastation*, though with nothing like the range (which did not matter too much in the Mediterranean), as well as being more heavily armed.

The armaments race went on with a further counter by

Britain in the building of *Inflexible*. And so it continued (as it always has) and in an almost never-ending spiral of increasing size and, of course, of cost. The guns for the Italian fleet were, incidentally, built by Armstrongs of Britain. As far back as the time of the Armada (when many of the Armada guns were British made) manufacturers of armaments necessarily sought sales wherever they could be found. Restrictions on the export of advanced armaments did not come into force among nations until this century — and even now, as has often been shown, were skilfully evaded, the profit motive being without a country.

So long as heavy guns were mostly muzzle loaders, and the science of gunnery control remained primitive, it was still expected that battles at sea would take place at close range, any long range work being done by fast torpedo boats equipped with the Whitehead torpedo. The great ships continued, therefore, to be built with the ram bow, something that was to survive into World War I and, despite the new developments that were to overtake all navies, this misinterpretation of events in the American Civil War and the Austro-Italian battle of Lissa continued to be applied by admiralties and naval architects in all countries. The end of the muzzle loader came with the perfecting of the interrupted screw, whereby the breech block on being closed was automatically locked. Like so many other things this was a French invention, but the firms of Armstrong and Whitworth were swift to move with improvements on the breech-loading mechanism, while at the same time Armstrong were also experimenting with something that would definitely end the long reign of the muzzle loader.

All explosive powders used in guns had customarily been quick burning, but by the 1880s slow burning powders had been introduced which changed the whole pattern of ordnance. With the slow-burning powder the reaction was prolonged, so that during the passage of the projectile down the bore of the gun something akin to a constant pressure behind it was maintained, thus giving a much higher muzzle velocity. Clearly, to achieve maximum effect with this type of powder a gun with a long bore is required and, with breech loaders, it was easier to increase the length since they did not suffer from the loading problems of muzzle loaders. Gradually also the old material, wrought iron, which had continued in use as a reinforcement over an inner steel tube gave place to steel throughout. Before the close of the century guns of immense power were possible and armour protection, however thick (and it had reached almost absurd densities), could never be considered invulnerable at anything approaching the ranges at which actions might now expect to be fought. Bernard Brodie in *Sea Power in the Machine Age* remarks:

> The 16.25 breech-loading gun of 1884, weighing 111 tons, had a power that would have been considered fanciful a decade earlier. It would hurl a projectile weighing 1800 pounds with a muzzle velocity of 2148 feet per second and a total energy of 57,580 foot tons, enabling it at 1000 yards to penetrate 34.1 inches of wrought iron.

The century concluded with two wars in both of which naval battles took place, but in neither of which could anything of real value be learned by the major naval powers. At the battle of the Yalu in 1894 between the Chinese and Japanese, the Chinese navy was almost entirely unskilled. Although they had two armoured coast defence battleships and three other semi-protected ironclads, they were quite unsuited to meet the Japanese who were very well trained and had a formidable number of modern protected cruisers, one British built the others French, and armed with the latest breech-loading, quick-firing guns. The triumph of the Japanese was not only the result of discipline and training, but of the quick-firing gun — one in which the recoil is automatically absorbed and the gun run back into the firing position, and where the ammunition is made up like a rifle bullet with projectile and charge in a brass cartridge case. Against the storm of fire that poured from these guns the Chinese had little chance, and the result was a foregone conclusion. One thing that was certainly demonstrated was the immense resisting power of the armoured ship. Had the Chinese been in possession of two modern battleships with properly trained crews, instead of their two out-of-date coastal defence armoured vessels, they would have been able to sink a number of Japanese cruisers before they ever got within range and certainly prevented their concerted attack. (Both the Chinese armour clads were hit over and over again by fire from the Japanese cruisers, yet their armour was never pierced.) Some western observers at the time missed this point and judged that sea battles of the future might possibly be fought between armoured heavy cruisers — these taking the place, as it were, of the 74s of the past. One thing that grabbed everybody's attention was that, in an astonishingly short space of time, Japan had changed from a medieval to a modern state. (There were even senior officers in her army and her navy who, in their youth, had fought samurai style, themselves in armour.) To the concern of not only China but all those others with interest in the area, a new naval power had suddenly arisen in the Far East.

The Spanish-American War of 1898, in which the battle of Santiago de Cuba occurred, merits mention in this account more for the fact that it brought to the attention of the Americans the necessity of maintaining an up-to-date and thoroughly efficient navy in the western hemisphere than for anything else. Curiously enough, since the United States navy had played so large a part in the Civil War, it had been badly neglected during the period that followed, and it was not until the late 1880s that the United States began the construction of a seagoing fleet such as a great power with long ocean seaboards clearly required. Even so, at the time that the war broke out with Spain over the Cuban question, many obsolete vessels were still in service and, to make good the numbers of its depleted navy, some liners had to be armed and other merchant navy ships used as auxiliaries. The result of the action off Santiago was the destruction of the Spanish fleet which was old and ineptly handled. Lessons that other naval powers could draw from this war were that gunnery had scarcely advanced — certainly as regards efficient control and direction — and that fire, due to the explosive nature of modern shells, remained the greatest hazard to ships. J. R. Hale, writing not long after the event, summed it up:

> It must be confessed that the gunnery of the Americans was not of a high order. Some 6,500 shells were expended during the action. The Spanish wrecks [which had run themselves aground] were carefully examined, and all hits counted. Fires and explosions perhaps obliterated the traces of some of them, but so far as could be ascertained, the hits on the hulls and the upper works were comparatively few.... The fact that three of the Spanish cruisers had been rendered helpless by fires lighted on board by shells accentuated the lesson already learned from the battle of the Yalu as to the necessity of eliminating inflammable material in the construction and fittings of warships.

So, with these two now almost forgotten naval actions, the long and comparatively peaceful years of the post-Trafalgar century drew to a close. The *Pax Britannica,* which had enabled so many new countries to develop their economies in peace and without expensive armaments, had been maintained very largely by the presence on the high seas of those great ships — untried in battle and their names forgotten save in the record books — which had provided the supreme evidence of power that does not need to be applied. Those who celebrated the *fin de siècle* in a mood of ostentatious melancholy could hardly have known that the century about to be born would wear the iron face of the god of war and be more terrible than any in recorded history.

CHAPTER NINE

The New Era Begins

Devastation had established a new era in ship design and, like *Revenge*, had set a mould that was to last. In this case, that in itself meant little more than twenty years, for with the rate of development in materials and techniques due to the Industrial Revolution changes came thick and fast. What had previously, with manpower, simple tools and traditional thinking, taken two centuries to alter to any great degree now occurred within decades: it was as if time itself had become foreshortened. Sail of course had completely disappeared in warships, but the Royal Navy's architects having achieved what seemed their breakthrough, tended to relapse into slumber. For this they cannot entirely be blamed, for their purpose of maintaining peace on the high seas and the security of trade routes throughout the British Empire had been achieved. There were as yet no apparent challengers and, true to its tradition of making no innovations unless forced to by another power, class after class followed much upon the lines of *Devastation*. The French and other powers seemed prepared to accept, or follow, this lead and, while the tonnage of ships rose greatly (up to displacements of 16,000 tons), the main changes were technical improvements giving higher speeds and increased penetration of shell fire. For a brief moment it seemed as if the seventeenth century had been followed by the eighteenth in a comfortable traditionalism.

The year 1900 itself was marked by the launching of a battleship by a hitherto little known naval power, a launching that might be viewed with hindsight as ominous.

Kaiser Barbarossa, of 11,150 tons displacement, marked the appearance of a formidable military power in Europe that had now turned to aspirations on the sea. Since the fall of Paris and the defeat of the French in 1870, to be followed by the unification of Germany, the power unleashed by Bismarck was not to be contained within the comparatively narrow bounds of Germany's seaboard. Imperial dreams — colonies as well as trade — meant that this new nation with all its scientific and industrial abilities would require a powerful navy. Admiral Alfred von Tirpitz, who had entered the Prussian navy in 1865, was the ideal man to continue Bismarck's train of thought at sea, and although conflict with Britain was always something that he resolutely rejected he saw clearly that a strong navy was necessary for a country such as Germany had become. The naval programme of 1900 included the building of 19 battleships, 6 large and 16 smaller cruisers, as well as a number of coastal defence ships, all within the next seven years. The *Kaiser Barbarossa* was typical of the new construction: with a length of 396 feet on a beam of 67 feet and a draught of 25.5 feet, she was armed with four 9½ inch guns in two turrets fore and aft, as well as fourteen 6 inch and fourteen 3½ inch in barbettes. Like most battleships of her period she was also armed with torpedo tubes and, in the manner of some French battleships, had three propellers which, with nearly 14,000 hp engines, could drive her at 18 knots.

The torpedo, which would play a considerable part in the first major naval encounter of the twentieth century, had become an object of dread to all naval powers, for it seemed that with its coming the great ship had become threatened as never before. No longer would a fleet action be fought against equals, but flotillas of small fast ships armed with torpedoes would strike from afar or sweep into harbours and anchorages destroying battle fleets where they lay. So great had this fear become that all major fleet bases began to take new measures for protection — torpedo-boat destroyers not only to protect the fleet but to maintain patrol outside its harbours, while in the British Mediterranean fleet base of

Malta a great new breakwater was constructed as much for protection from torpedoes fired from seawards as against winter storms.

Torpedo netting was designed (in principle somewhat like the knight's chain mail of old) to be lowered from booms to form a curtain round the sides of the ship. Effective enough at anchor but totally useless if the great ship was intended to proceed to sea and carry out normal evolutions, it was later to be superseded by bulges externally built onto the ship's real lines and subdivided into many compartments so as to absorb a torpedo's explosion. These of course considerably reduced a ship's speed and since, till the end of World War II, all torpedoes left a visible wake, the most common practice was for ships to turn towards or away from torpedoes, thus presenting the minimum profile.

The Russo-Japanese war which broke out in 1904 was to demonstrate the importance both of the torpedo and the mine in all future warfare, and was to prove the most important event in naval history since the great ship had become armoured, equipped with rifled guns firing shells, and steam-propelled. In the initial phases of the war it was destroyers armed with torpedoes that achieved the most effect against capital ships; ten Japanese destroyers attacking the Russian Far East fleet anchored in Port Arthur, two of the Russian battleships being hit and seriously damaged as well as one large cruiser. If the Japanese had had more experience in the use of torpedoes they might indeed have sunk the whole Russian squadron, which was lying inadequately protected and with no safety precautions taken against such an attack. Unluckily for the Russians only a few days later they were to lose their only able admiral, Makaroff, in his flagship, the battleship *Petropaulovsk*, when a Japanese mine exploded beneath her, setting off her torpedo compartment, her magazines and her boilers; she sank within two minutes. The Russians were to suffer another battleship disabled by a mine, while the Japanese for their part were to lose two battleships to mines during this phase of action off Port Arthur. The future importance of the lowly minesweeper was demonstrated, as well as the inadequacy of underwater protection for battleships. With the surrender of Port Arthur the whole of the remaining Russian Far East fleet fell into Japanese hands.

In one of the most amazing fleet movements in history — unparalleled previously in the age of steam — Russia now proceeded to move almost the whole of her Baltic fleet to the Far East (her fleet from the Black Sea could not pass through the Dardanelles on account of international treaties). It sailed in two main divisions, Admiral Rodzhestvenski in command proceeding via West Africa to the Far East with the first division, and the second division going through the Mediterranean and the Suez Canal. It took seven months for the whole fleet to assemble in the East. Their aim was to reach Vladivostok — but without a battle if possible. The fleet consisted of seven battleships, two armoured cruisers, some protected vessels and a number of torpedo-boat destroyers. Along with them went a miscellaneous collection of colliers, store ships, hospital and repair ships. Even so, if it had not been for the indulgent eye of France, permitting these belligerents to use coaling depots in French colonies on the way, it would never have been possible with the supply train available at the time to move so many men and so many heavy ships from one end of the earth to another: it was a revelation as to what might be achieved in any future conflicts. Inevitably after so long a voyage, without access to dockyard facilities, mechanical defects were much in evidence and the ships themselves were foul from an accumulation of underwater parasites like barnacles. The Russians could not make anything like their full speed when it came to the final dash for Vladivostok, while the Japanese waited for them fresh from their home bases.

Admiral Togo who commanded the Japanese fleet was inferior in numbers, with four battleships, eight armoured cruisers and a number of protected craft as well as torpedo boats. On the other hand, only five of the Russian battleships were modern, one hardly deserved to lie in the battle line. Furthermore, as in the battle of the Yalu against China,

Japan possessed in her cruisers equipped with their quick-firing gun vessels that were a match for all except modern battleships. Furthermore, awaiting battle off their own shores, Togo could call upon several auxiliary squadrons, out of date but quite capable of fighting, and a number of destroyers as well as even more torpedo boats. Admiral Rodzhestvenski for his part was faced at the end of months of long voyage with the speed of his ships reduced (due to the disadvantages mentioned) and without at any time having the opportunity to exercise his fleet together or prepare any tactical plan.

Captain Semenoff who was aboard the Russian flagship during the action that was to follow voiced his feelings: '…we were forcibly reminded of the old truism that a "fleet" is created by long practice at sea in time of peace (cruising, not remaining in port), and that a collection of ships of various types hastily collected, which have only learned to sail together on the way to the theatre of operations, is no fleet, but a chance concourse of vessels.'

The Russian battleships were also overloaded with coal, Rodzheventski having decided to leave most of the colliers and other store ships in the mouth of the Yang-tse river, while the fleet passed through the Tsu-shima straits headed for Vladivostok. Whichever of three available routes that the Russians could have taken, all would bring them within easy reach of the Japanese, operating from their home bases. The Russians knew in their hearts that the best that could happen was for thick weather and heavy seas to enable them to slip through without any major close encounter with the enemy.

An interesting feature of the action was that this was the first occasion in which wireless telegraphy had been used in warfare, the Russians, who were anxious to conceal their position, maintaining wireless silence, while the Japanese felt free to organize their divisions by wireless, so that once contact had been made their main battle fleet could be summoned. In this as in all else they had the advantage, and once one of their cruisers had sighted the enemy shortly after daybreak there was no chance of the Russians 'slipping through unobserved'. Throughout the morning of 27 May 1905 Japanese cruiser squadrons kept their watch, veering away as soon as the Russians on one occasion opened fire at a range of over five miles. Admiral Rodzhestvenski had altered course direct for Vladivostok and rightly surmised that the main body of the Japanese fleet was gathering in the straits ahead of him. Admiral Togo, in fact, in order to cover the available approaches to the Sea of Japan had kept his battlefleet at anchor off the mainland of Korea and had steered eastward on receiving the first report of the Russians' position, so as to lay himself just north of the island of Tsu-Tshima.

The Russians advancing in line ahead now suffered the worst tactical blow that could have befallen them, for the Japanese with their superior speed were able to complete the manoeuvre known as 'crossing the T' — bringing their line across the bows of the Russian battleship division so that the converging fire of their ships could be concentrated on the leading Russian ships. Any conception that fleet engagements would in the future be determined by torpedoes rather than guns was soon dispelled for, even as the Russians began to turn so as to bring their own line into action, the first Japanese shells started to hit. The Japanese were using a new type of shell with a more sensitive fuse which, Captain Semenoff observed, 'burst at the slightest obstacle — even a funnel guy or a boat derrick'. This in itself might have proved ineffective when confronted with armoured sides, but the fact that the Russians were overloaded with coal, some of it stored above the armoured decks, meant that fires began to break out on ship after ship as they were hit. Although the Russians were not slow to get the Japanese range, their enemy had better armour and of course were not encumbered, nor, like the Russians, generally overloaded as they had necessarily been for their long passage. Even if it had not been for the superb skill shown by Admiral Togo and his disciplined crews the result might have been foreseen as inevitable — a massive defeat for the Russians and a victory of unparalleled consequence for the Japanese. At the conclusion of the day's action four Russian battleships had been sunk and a number of other ships damaged, while the only major Japanese damage had been to an armoured ship which had been forced to leave the line with her rudder disabled, but which was still capable of rejoining later in the day. A hundred years after Trafalgar Admiral Togo had secured a victory in every way as decisive as had Nelson. Throughout the night that followed, while ordering all his heavy ships to keep clear of the fleeing enemy, Togo sent in his flotillas of torpedo boats. The overall battle had been won by gunnery, but its conclusion was to lie with the torpedo. The only ships of the whole Russian fleet to reach Vladivostok were two destroyers and one fast light cruiser.

Quite apart from the unusual circumstances of this battle, certain conclusions were inevitably drawn by warship designers and constructors, as well as the navies of other powers. The first was that the battleship remained the dominant force afloat and that major fleet actions were still decided by gunnery — at long ranges. The accuracy of naval gunnery, something that had been hitherto somewhat neglected, became paramount. Nelson's old adage, 'No captain can do very wrong who places his ship alongside that of an enemy', clearly had no place in the twentieth century. Another thing demonstrated was the inaccuracy of torpedo fire, which it had been feared would come to dominate a fleet action. Many salvoes of torpedoes had been fired during the night attacks by Togo's vessels and relatively few hits scored, while at the same time the modern quick-firing gun was clearly capable of giving protection against torpedo-boat attacks. (It was also observed that ships which had not illuminated their attackers overnight seemed to have a better chance of escaping than those which switched on their searchlights.) The superior speed of the Japanese had been in evidence throughout and even though this was largely due to the long period that the Russians had spent at sea it was seen that speed above all had produced the tactical advantage. Siegfried Breyer

in *Battleships and Battle Cruisers* remarks: 'The dangers
inherent in the conventional battleship also revealed
themselves as a warning. This applied particularly to the
dangers resulting from poor stability, low seaworthiness
and inadequate underwater protection.' The latter problem
would never — and could never — be satisfactorily solved,
but the high profile of the Russian ships had clearly made
them an easier target than the Japanese, which had very
largely followed the design of Britain's battleships, and in
particular the style of *Devastation*. As in the case of the
battle of Lissa in the Austro-Italian war it was shown once
again, and indeed eternally, that nothing is more important
than highly trained officers and crews who are accustomed
to working together.

The result of the war was that Japan, having established
a dominant place in the East, began a great expansion of
her navy — first of all repairing and rearming the Russian
ships that had been captured at Tsu-Tshima and secondly
with a new building programme of her own. Within a
period of two years they would have laid down two giant
battleships of nearly 20,000 tons displacement, bigger than
any others in the world. The United States, inevitably casting
uneasy glances in the direction of the Pacific, were likewise
impelled to devote much expenditure to the building of new
battleships and cruiser squadrons. There was an uneasy
stirring throughout the world, as if quite unconsciously
nations and their rulers were becoming aware that some
changes of balance was taking place and that the long period
of tranquillity (broken only by distant wars) was coming to
an end.

Some years before the navies of the world began
concentrating on building larger battleships, giving priority
to their gunnery and the means of improving it, and
researching into optical instruments for gunnery controls,
a small vessel had made its appearance which was to shake
the whole fabric upon which these navies were built. In the
full pomp and circumstance of Queen Victoria's Diamond
Jubilee in 1897, among the almost interminable lines of

the British fleet paraded off Spithead, flags flying over all
the masts and funnels and banks of guns, an intruder had
penetrated. This was an irritating, small, very fast boat
which, like a wasp at a dignified tea party, kept buzzing
past the huge dowager-like ships and intruding into areas
which were prohibited to all except the great and the noble.
The worst thing was that the Royal Navy did not appear to
have a single vessel capable of chasing it away. Sir Charles
Parsons had arrived in his *Turbinia,* the first turbine-driven
ship.

Sir Charles, proprietor of the Parsons Marine Steam
Turbine Company of Wallsend-on-Tyne, was made a
Fellow of the Royal Society in the following year, received
numerous other honorary degrees and medals in his lifetime
and was awarded the Order of Merit in his later years. At
the time of the Queen's Jubilee he felt that his invention
of the steam turbine engine had been virtually ignored by
the Admiralty and he sought in this spectacular fashion to
draw attention to its considerable advantages over the steam
reciprocating engine which still drove all the units of the
fleet. The latter had shown its worth for very many years
now, but even its most ardent advocates were forced to admit
that the maximum speed of a reciprocating engine could not
be maintained for many hours, and that at speeds above
14 knots it was practically impossible to maintain a fleet
steaming in formation. There was not a fleet in the world
with reciprocating engines that could maintain top speed for
as long as eight hours without an engine breaking down in
one or more of its units. At high speeds it would be found
that the turbine engine used less coal than a reciprocating
engine, produced more power for engine weight, and was
not similarly subject to breakdowns. Sir Charles Parsons, by
his very unVictorian display in 1897, had managed to force
a startled Admiralty to take notice of his invention. The
result was that, not long afterwards, an order was placed for
two turbine-driven destroyers, one of which was to achieve
speeds of more than 37 knots.

What remained to be seen, and what was of utmost

importance at that moment at the beginning of the twentieth century, was whether the steam turbine, which had shown its efficiency for small boats and ships at high speeds, could ever be accommodated to something as large as a battleship. And this was the all-important question of the moment, especially since the Russo-Japanese War seemed to have confirmed the place of the battleship in any major fleet engagements of the future. Even before the events of Tsu-Tshima the Americans had ordered battleships of 18,000 tons, and this size was to be exceeded in the future as secondary armament of heavy guns began to be added to the initial heavy armament. At the same time there were those who could see that the time was coming when the 'all big one calibre gun battleship' would dominate everything else on the oceans of the world. The reason for this was the steady improvement in optical instruments, considerable development in gunlaying equipment, and the modernization of both firing and observation methods. Once these had reached an almost equally high standard the heavy secondary armament would be no more than a source of irritation and confusion — particularly when it came to spotting the fall of salvoes — since the secondary armament would raise shell splashes that would prevent the director from recognizing which was the fall of shot from the main armament.

At HMS *Excellent,* the naval gunnery school at Portsmouth, advances were being made to elevate gunnery from a crude and imprecise method of damaging the enemy into as near an exact science as possible. This was largely the work of Sir Percy Scott and his staff who, among a number of other reforms, had introduced the system of 'director' firing — something which was essential if the main armament was to strike the target all in one coordinated blow. In this system a trained gunnery officer, situated high up in a special position on the foremast, had under his control the optical rangefinder and gunnery director. With these he directed the ship's main armament — his director sight being connected with the turrets by an electrical circuit. As soon as his sight, and therefore the guns, were correctly on target the officer pressed a button which completed the circuit and fired the guns at the same time. Allowance was made for the distance apart of the various turrets, and at a later date all the information fed to the guns and to the director was worked out at a transmitting station, secure in a protected area. A similar arrangement was also to be made for the heavy secondary armament, but even before this had been effected it had become clear that the great battleship should be confined to all 'big gun' main armament alone.

The Germans had been the first to adopt the conception of an 'all big, one calibre gun battleship' in the late nineteenth century, and their ideas were acknowledged by Vittorio Cuniberti in his design which he submitted to the Admiralty and called 'an ideal battleship for the Royal Navy'. This had a displacement of 17,000 tons (more than the navy had built before) twelve 12-inch quick-firing guns and eighteen 3-inch quick-firing guns, and was to have a speed of 24 knots. The armour and the guns were easy enough for Britain to produce, but such a speed was unobtainable with the conventional reciprocating engines.

It so happened that the turn of the century saw a most unusual Commander-in-Chief of the British Mediterranean fleet — a man who had long been attracted towards the idea of an all big one calibre gun battlefleet. This was Admiral Lord Fisher, a man of very independent views and character, who was destined to rattle more senior officers and disturb more naval shibboleths than any before or since. In October 1904 Fisher was appointed First Sea Lord, and he at once established a 'Committee on Designs' to which he appointed eight naval officers and eight civilians (scientists, industrialists and engineers). To them was given the task of defining the design principles of two types of modern warships — firstly, an 'all big gun battleship' and secondly a modern armoured cruiser. Fisher had read the lessons to be derived from the Far East, and he had also determined to do something that was quite contrary to that old-established British naval policy of not being the first to initiate a new move. He and his committee worked furiously together and finally came up with the most important thing first of all — the new battleship. Furthermore, unlike all previous new designs built by any navies (where it was commonplace to invite other naval powers to see what you had on the stocks), this ship was to be built very quickly and in total secrecy — speed in itself being essential to ensure secrecy. Fisher's aim was to steal a march on all the other powers, particularly Germany whose new navy he had had his eye on for a long time, and to obtain a lead over them so that by the time they had begun to follow, Britain would be even further advanced on an improved version.

Building a great ship had always been a slow and considered matter, befitting its nature as well as the capital expenditure involved. All was now to be changed, naturally to the disgust of those who favoured the old way, but equally to the advantage of Fisher's idea — even though this new approach did inevitably spur on the arms race that was to end in such disaster for Europe. The keel of the new battleship was laid at Portsmouth (not remote from the building place of *Mary Rose)* on 2 October 1905 and — beating his own record of two years for the construction of a capital ship — Fisher saw to it that the new ship was complete and even ready for her trials exactly a year and a day afterwards.

Dreadnought was to give her name to a whole class of warships which were to follow her worldwide. The first 'all big one calibre gun battleship' to be commissioned, she had ten 12-inch guns mounted in five turrets, three in the centre line and two on the sides so that six guns could be fired forward, six aft, and eight on the broadside. She also had a number of small quick-firing guns mounted on top of the turrets, the superstructure and the quarterdeck, for repelling torpedo boat attacks. In common with other battleships of her time she had five underwater torpedo tubes. But quite apart from her armament, *Dreadnought* was distinguished from all other battleships by the fact that she had turbine engines, Sir Charles Parsons himself having backed Lord Fisher over the design and having guaranteed that his firm could build turbines of sufficient size to drive a battleship. *Dreadnought* had four of them driving four propellers, with eighteen boilers designed to burn oil as well as coal — another first. Since such a ship was entirely designed with long range, big gun action in mind, the ram, which had become a feature of the battleship for so long, through a general misreading of the battle of Lissa, was dispensed with by *Dreadnought* and her class. Her barbettes were made of 11-inch armour and 11-inch armour also covered her amidships, fining down towards the bows and stern to 6-4 inches thick. She was 527 feet long by 82 feet on the beam, with a draught of 26 feet, and displacing 17,900 tons. On her trials she managed over 22 knots but she was rated at a speed of 21 knots, as such being the fastest battleship in the Royal Navy. The speed and secrecy with which *Dreadnought* had been built certainly paid off in terms of surprising the rest of the naval world, but in doing so Fisher's conception had exactly the effect that the Royal Navy had striven to avoid throughout all the years; it started off a stampede of great ship building, any country which considered itself of big power status on the seas emulating the British example. Germany, for instance, laid down two 'dreadnoughts' in the year that the original was launched, and France as well as the United States followed hard on their heels. Although the Americans were to build far larger ships, and even more heavily armed, they were hardly regarded as formidable as those built by Germany, nor in view of the political climate were they viewed as in any way representing such a threat to Britain's command of the seas.

Contributory to the whole atmosphere prior to the outbreak of World War I — the colonial aspirations of European powers, the machinations of politicians, trade and industrial rivalries, and the terrible cat's cradle of monarchies and treaties — was undoubtedly the proliferation of great ship building that now seized the powers.

CHAPTER TEN

Onward — to Stalemate

Larger and larger grew the ships, heavier and heavier their armour, greater and greater the weight of metal that they could hurl for miles across the sea. It seemed as if there was no end to the expenditure which governments were prepared to lavish upon the great ship. Noteworthy about the German capital ships that followed *Dreadnought* was something that was to distinguish all such German ships during the years to come — their greater beam and their honeycomb style of subdivided interior. Germany, which did not have to maintain long imperial sea links or build ships as suitable for the tropics as the north, could concentrate on ships designed mainly for forays into the North Sea. Unlike the British, who would be compelled to make their main fleet base the cold and inhospitable Scapa Flow in the Orkney islands, the Germans could return to Kiel and other home ports, and sailors when not engaged at sea could be housed in comfortable barracks. This meant that their battleships not only had far more effective torpedo bulkheads than any other navy, but that living space areas could be subdivided to a degree which sailors, who had truly to live in their ships for months on end, would have found intolerable. The resulting German Dreadnoughts, the *Nassau* class, displacing 18,900 tons, were slightly shorter and beamier than *Dreadnought*, had armour half an inch thicker, and were capable of slightly under 21 knots. In place of the British ten 12-inch they mounted twelve 11-inch guns. Ballistically only slightly inferior, these well-tested German guns were considered by Tirpitz to be adequate for any actions that might take place in the North Sea — an area where visibility is usually poor and where, therefore, long-range engagaments were unlikely.

More carefully thought out than Fisher's *Dreadnought* because of the time intervening, the *Nassau* class was immediately to disprove Fisher's belief that Germany would never be able to match the British shipbuilding industry. At one blow the whole theory on which his great idea had been based was shattered. In 1908 a supplementary naval building law in Germany ensured that by 1914 Germany would have in the front line sixteen capital ships and five battle cruisers. The latter were yet another of Fisher's ideas, with which he hoped to put paid to the threat of fast cruisers (such as those which Japan had deployed against China and Russia) against Britain's trade lifelines in the event of an international war. The Japanese themselves had already shown the way in 1905 with *Tsukuba* of 15,000 tons, having a cruiser hull and mounting four 12-inch guns as well as twelve 6-inch.

The first British battle cruiser (for which the name was coined) was *Invincible,* launched in 1907 and — like *Dreadnought* — ready for trials a year later. She was longer, 567 feet, but otherwise outwardly not dissimilar, having eight 12-inch guns in turrets, two on the centre line and one on each side. Her great difference lay in her armour for, in order to reduce weight to give the necessary speed, she had only 7 inches of armour as against *Dreadnought's* 11 inches. Speed, which was expected to give the battle cruiser her protection, was provided by turbines developing 41,000 hp driving four propellers and giving her on trials 26.5 knots. The original and main purpose of battle cruisers of the Invincible class was for them to be able to overtake the enemy's fast cruisers and to out-range them. A secondary consideration which later developed was for the battle cruisers to proceed in advance of the Grand Fleet, locate the enemy fleet and hang on to it until such time as the Grand Fleet came up, when they would take station ahead until both main fleets were engaged in a major action.

They proved their worth in the first requirement during the battle of the Falkland Islands in December 1914, when

Invincible and her sister ship *Inflexible* destroyed the German cruisers *Scharnhorst* and *Gneisenau*. Such opportunities to use battle cruisers did not recur, however, and in their second role it was shown that they were unsuitable. The losses of British battle cruisers at Jutland revealed that their lack of sufficient armour made them unfitted for the battle line — a fact which should have surprised nobody, though it did. These beautiful looking ships, their length giving them an elegance that the heavier battleship could never have, remind one inevitably of that distant ancestor, the galleasse. They were a hybrid between the battleship and the cruiser just as the galleasse was a hybrid between the galleon and the galley. But whereas at Lepanto the galleasses, thrown forward by Don John of Austria, broke up the Turkish formation and contributed to victory, the battle cruisers advanced at Jutland themselves fell victims. Both the galleon and the battleship survived throughout their eras because they could take punishment just as much as give it. The exotic hybrids perished for lack of that all-important quality, endurance.

Siegfried Breyer in *Battleships and Battle Cruisers* summed up the basic position occasioned by the British move to build the 'Dreadnoughts', the battle cruisers, and all that followed them:

The United Kingdom had no doubt gained a considerable lead at first; however, when Germany followed suit and built similar ships it soon became obvious that the numerous older British ships had been devalued as a result. During the 1890s the Royal Navy had secured a remarkable superiority of which it was justly proud. For example, from 1889, when the Naval Defence Act came into force, until 1905 it had built a total of 46 battleships compared with 24 German ones. If one excludes the oldest ones, i.e. all those built before 1893, this resulted in a ratio of 40 British to 20 German.... The United Kingdom had paid insufficient attention to other navies, especially Germany's, by devaluing its substantial numbers of battleships and armoured cruisers. To maintain its lead, the United Kingdom was now forced to place orders for increasingly large and powerful ships only to find itself constantly under pressure in the course of development when other navies, especially the German navy, followed suit. The construction of these instruments of power imposed considerable financial strains upon the United Kingdom. The other navies, which had up to then found themselves in a hopeless position, were thus given the chance to make a fresh start. From the point of view of power politics, the development of the *Dreadnought* and *Invincible* proved a singularly inefficient instrument.

It is difficult to disagree with this judgement and, with the aid of hindsight, it would seem that Fisher's bold innovations, and his breaking of the navy's old rule of making no advance unless compelled to, were at fault. Certainly they led to the great naval arms race, super-Dreadnoughts succeeding Dreadnoughts from 1909 onwards. The tonnage mounted from the original *Dreadnought*'s 17,900 to the 30,000 tons of the *Queen Elizabeth* class battleships, the first of which was laid down in 1912. Capable of 25 knots (as fast as the first battle cruisers), armed with eight 15-inch guns mounted in four centre-line turrets (two forward and two aft), they combined the speed of battle cruisers with the armour of battleships (13 inches amidships) and burned oil fuel only. *Queen Elizabeth, Barham, Malaya, Valiant* and *Warspite* were without doubt the foremost class of battleships ever built, not because there were never battleships both larger, faster and more heavily-gunned than them, but because they saw service in both world wars, playing an important part in both, and were also the most profitable in their service return on capital investment of any in history. Only *Barham* was sunk in war, being torpedoed by a U-boat off the Egyptian coast in November 1941. The other four all survived many actions, including Jutland, and damage from shells, mines, torpedoes and aircraft bombs during two World Wars, to end by being scrapped in their home country after World

War II. Few ships can ever have seen more service or earned more battle honours.

During these vast building programmes prior to World War I it seems, looking back, as if all countries — but particularly Britain and Germany — were indeed trying to astonish one another with the prodigious appearance and size of their ships. The United States, France, Italy and Japan were building equally large — if not so many — capital ships, but they do not occupy the foreground of history since they were never to be seen in the harsh and exposing light of battle. Even if considerably less successful than the *Queen Elizabeth* class ships, the British *Lion, Princess Royal* and *Queen Mary* mark the apogee of the great ship in its line of succession from the ship of the line and great carrack. Affectionately termed in the navy 'splendid cats', these super battle cruisers deserved their name although, in company with the battle cruisers that had preceded them, they suffered from similar defects.

Lion, which was to be Admiral Beatty's flagship at Jutland, was the first of her class and was ready for trials in 1908. She was larger than the largest battleships, with a displacement of nearly 30,000 tons (so far and so fast had things developed). She was 700 feet long, 88 feet on the beam, and had a draught of 28.9 feet. With four Parsons turbines driving four propellers she developed 70,000 hp, giving her a speed of 27 knots, faster than any other large ship in the world. Her main armament consisted of eight 13.5 inch guns in four twin turrets, all mounted in the centre line of the ship. Following other foreign navies, led by the United States, it had been found that greater stability (leading to greater accuracy) was achieved by having all the main armament in the centre. In common with the battle cruisers that preceded her, *Lion* and her sister ships had less armour than the battleships, 9 inches at the most, fining down to 6-4 inches at bows and stern. With the sweep of her forward guns up to the bridge, the single rod mast and the hunched shoulders of the direct control tower, she achieved an impression of great power and grace — the latter quality very evident when seen beam on where her lines could be fully appreciated. Such ships are rare in the history of great naval vessels, and their likes would not be seen again.

Germany, not to be outdone, responded with *Derfflinger* and her sister ships, *Lützow* and *Hindenburg*. Launched in 1913 she was ready just in time for the war, in which she distinguished herself more than any of the other battle cruisers. *Derfflinger* marked the changeover of the German navy to 12-inch calibre guns and her main armament consisted of eight of these in four twin turrets set in the centre line. She had heavier plating, however, than *Lion* and her class, 12 inches at the waterline and 10-11 inches round barbettes and turrets, but was slightly slower, her 63,000 hp engines giving her a speed of 26.5 knots. Six hundred and eighty nine feet long, 95 feet on the beam, with a draught of 27 feet, she displaced just over 26,000 tons and was undoubtedly one of the most graceful of these leviathans ever built, with her long forecastle and her gently rising sheer. Meanwhile the Russians, French, Austrians, Italians and Americans had also begun to build ships of the *Dreadnought* type, but these were distinguished from the German and British by setting their main armament in triple as opposed to twin turrets.

In 1890 Lord Salisbury had made a very great error in policy, which like many such did not appear of importance at the time. He had ceded to Germany the island of Heligoland in the North Sea which England had held since the beginning of the eighteenth century. Lying off the mouths of the Elbe and the Weser and only twenty eight miles from the nearest point of the mainland, it had appeared of little value and in return Salisbury had obtained the waiving by Germany of some claims on the obviously valuable island of Zanzibar. But only two years before this, Kaiser William II had begun his reign in Germany and the young ruler had already indicated that he had repudiated Bismarck's policy of keeping the German empire within Europe. The latter had declared that colonies 'would only be a source of weakness, because they could only be defended by powerful fleets, and Germany's geographical position does not necessitate her development into a first-class maritime power'. The building of the great new German navy was, starting in ambitious terms from 1900, also accompanied by the conversion of Heligoland from an obscure fishing island into a massive fortress with great breakwaters that formed a fine advanced harbour, capable of sheltering Germany's new navy behind barriers of minefields and protected by large coastal batteries. The island had in fact become like a gun pointed at the heart of England, and it was this hardly concealed threat which had, perhaps, largely provoked Fisher's response — leading in its turn to the whole escalation of the naval arms race.

Even while World War I was becoming visible like a thunder cloud on the horizon, further developments of the industrial age were taking place — developments that would ultimately remove the great ship from its dominant position, as surely as the gun and the efficient sailing ship had removed the galley. Communications were being drastically altered by wireless telegraphy, which the Japanese had first made use of in the battle of Tsu-Tshima, and the ability to transmit information and orders over great distances meant that the independent command was coming to an end and, in these early stages, added to the complexity — and the confusion — of controlling major fleet operations. (Inefficient use of communications was to prove one of Britain's major weaknesses in the battle of Jutland.)

Both the mine and the torpedo, as had been seen in the Far Eastern wars, posed great threats to battleships, and mines as developed by Britain and Germany were to play a major part in World War I, quite apart from sinking enemy ships, in determining what areas of the sea were available for use at any time. Submarines, from their early beginnings in the American Civil War, had now become really efficient warships and the danger to great ships lay more with torpedoes launched from submarines than from attacks by torpedo boats. So much more had to be thought about and so much more had to be guarded against. As yet, the major revolution in naval warfare had hardly declared itself.

Only on the horizon, and visible to the most far sighted of eyes, was the primitive aircraft detectable as the machine that would ultimately remove the great battleship from the world scene.

As with the submarine so with aircraft, it was the Americans who had first attempted its use in conjunction with naval ships. As early as 1910 a 'flying machine' had managed to take off (and reach the shore) from a special platform built on the forecastle of a US Navy cruiser. Perhaps because they did not see any necessity, such as a war generates, the Americans proceeded little further, even though the same 'bold aviator', Eugene Ely, managed not only to take off from, but also to land on a specially constructed platform built on a battleship. The British followed suit and in 1913 fitted the cruiser *Hermes* with a flying deck, but the impracticality with the aircraft at that time of being able to use them operationally, with the ship under way, both taking off and landing on, led the early Naval Air Service to feel that there was little future in wheeled aircraft. The seaplane clearly presented more opportunity for fleet use, both for spotting enemy movements and for bombing or torpedo dropping. Seaplanes could be hoisted into the water by cranes and hoisted back again when their mission was complete. *Hermes* herself was torpedoed in the first year of the war, but the Admiralty took over a number of packet boats for use as seaplane carriers. One of these, *Engadine,* was with the Grand Fleet at Jutland when the pilot was the first in history to report the sighting of enemy ships. (The fact that his message was never transmitted to Admirals Jellicoe and Beatty is in itself evidence of the inefficiency of the Royal Navy's signalling system which was to bedevil the battle.) During the First World War some ships were converted for use as real aircraft carriers, taking wheeled planes, and before it was over the Royal Navy possessed three of these — the first navy in the world to be so equipped.

When asked not long before war did break out in 1914 what he imagined a future great sea battle would be like Lord Fisher had replied, 'No one knows or can know until it comes.' To the people ashore in both Britain and on the Continent, after so long a period of peace, no one could envisage what any aspect of the war would be like — more particularly in Britain where the inhabitants had been constantly sheltered behind an all-powerful navy from the militarism that had now for some time been prominent all over Europe. In Britain the soldier was not a respected figure generally speaking (as Kipling's stories and ballads make clear), but the sailor had been viewed for so long as the country's saviour and shield that almost impossible things were expected of him — a great instant victory, for example, that would once and for ever silence the insolent Germans, bringing peace and order to all those quarrelling foreigners on the continent.

The great fleet action that the British public expected eluded them for two years after the war began and when it did come it proved, on the surface at least, so anticlimactic that there was a deep sense of disappointment and even dismay. The fact that the Royal Navy had swept from the seas within the first few months of the war all the enemy cruisers on the oceans of the world and had fought two important fleet actions in the battles of Coronel and Falklands were forgotten. That it consistently kept open the trade routes of the Empire and shepherded the unbroken flow of troopships between Britain and France were achievements that were so accepted as to pass almost unnoticed. Brought up for generations on a legendary Nelson, the people had expected something equally dramatic, having the effect of ending the war instantly — which of course Nelson's victories in themselves had never done.

The German High Seas Fleet, excellent though it was, had never been expected to meet the British Grand Fleet in a single decisive action. Their aim, which was successfully carried out during the first years, was to keep the main part of the Grand Fleet concentrated, while endeavouring, if it could, to lure detachments of it within range of a sudden major stroke from out of the fortress of Heligoland and the minefields off the Frisian coast. The German battle cruisers, in view of their speed, were favoured for what became known as 'tip-and-run raids' on the British mainland and it was naturally their British counterparts that tended to be sent south to try to catch them. In one of these ventures, known as the battle of the Dogger Bank, battle cruisers under Admiral Beatty came up with a reconnoitring force of battle cruisers under Admiral Hipper. The Germans were not seeking action and were naturally unaware that much of German naval signals were being read at the British Admiralty and it was in this way that Beatty had managed to find them. In the brief action that followed, before the German scouting squadron managed to make their escape, their flagship *Seydlitz* was badly damaged and another battle cruiser, *Blücher,* was sunk, while Beatty's flagship, *Lion,* leading the British line, was sufficiently damaged to be put out of action. Little was learned on the British side from this first encounter in the North Sea, but the Germans had learned one important lesson in design which the British were only to find out at terrible cost at Jutland. The main cause of *Blücher's* sinking and of Hipper's badly damaged *Seydlitz* was the same — flash from shell bursts which had swept through turrets and passed on to set fire to waiting charges. Having learned from this the Germans fitted flash doors to the turrets of their ships which opened only for the passage of shells and charges to the hoists. In this brief action, both sides deploying for the first time the great new ships which were the culmination of the arms race, it is interesting to note that Beatty's *Lion* opened fire on *Blücher* at a range of 11 miles — a far cry indeed from all the many point-blank battles that had been fought around the British Isles by other great ships of previous centuries.

In 1916 Admiral Scheer took over command of the German High Seas Fleet and within a short space of time had shown that a somewhat less static policy was to be adopted, battle cruisers being sent in that April to bombard the British coastal ports of Lowestoft and Yarmouth. As his Memoirs written after the war make clear, it was never his intention to provoke a decisive major fleet battle, but to use such irritating and — for the British public — demoralizing raids to lure an important detachment of Admiral Jellicoe's fleet south and bring against it a major part of the High Seas Fleet. It is possible he hoped that by one or two successful actions with heavier forces against lesser, and by a steady erosion by submarines of British capital ships, he might reduce the preponderance of the Grand Fleet to a point where he could one day engage it on something like equal terms.

At the end of May 1916 Scheer planned for Admiral Hipper's five battle cruisers to make for the entrance to the Skagerrak strait between Jutland and Norway, with a view to capturing any British shipping on the Baltic trade route. He knew that this move would inevitably produce a reaction and he hoped to lure a large detachment, most probably the British battle cruisers, in that direction. Meanwhile behind Hipper's battle cruisers Scheer himself would follow with the main body of the High Seas Fleet, keeping some forty miles away to the south. Unaware that the British Admiralty were, even if indifferently, picking up his signals Scheer could not know that his recent radio traffic had alerted them as to some major move about to be made. At the same time as ordering Beatty's battle cruiser squadron, reinforced by the 5th Battle squadron of the *Queen Elizabeth* class, towards the Danish coast, orders were sent to Admiral Jellicoe to take the whole Grand Fleet to sea. Beatty was to steer for a point north of the Dogger Bank, about one hundred miles from the Danish coast, after which he was to turn north and join the Grand Fleet as it came down towards him. By midnight on 30 May all these forces were at sea. As far as the Grand Fleet was concerned the whole operation resembled many others that had occurred in the past, and which usually ended with all the ships returning to their base having seen nothing more hostile than the drab expanse of the North Sea. On one thing Jellicoe had been misinformed — the Admiralty was continuing to receive messages from Scheer's flagship as if they came from his base at Wilhelmshaven and had told him that the main enemy fleet still appeared to be in the

Jade. In fact, Scheer had transferred his flagship's call sign to a powerful signalling station on shore — a deception that took in the British interception service.

On 2.15 p.m. on 31 May — a clear day with a calm sea — Beatty made the signal for his ships to turn to the north as arranged for his rendezvous with the Grand Fleet, his scouting screens of light cruisers covering his movements to the east and south. Hipper with his battle cruiser squadron was at this time some twenty miles to the eastward and Beatty's alteration of course meant that the two forces were now on converging courses. The cruiser *Galatea* was the first to report a German destroyer to the east and opened fire on her at 2.20 p.m. — the first shot of the day. Soon afterwards she sighted further destroyers and light cruisers, clearly the screen of a fleet, and signalled the news to Beatty and Jellicoe.

The Grand Fleet which was at cruising stations now raised full steam and turned to join Beatty's squadrons. Noticeable throughout the battle of Jutland was the inefficiency of British signalling, as two early examples show. The Battle Squadron of the fast *Queen Elizabeth* class had failed to read Beatty's first signal to turn north and take station five miles astern of his battle cruisers. Before the signal was repeated by light and they had time to turn and follow, as well as increase their speed to twenty-four knots (the speed at which the battle cruisers were now steaming), they were ten miles astern. A typical North Sea haze was now beginning to creep over the sea and a seaplane was sent up from *Engadine,* the converted Channel steamer which was with Beatty's squadrons. It was now that this all important observer's report transmitted sometime after 3 p.m. giving the nature and course of the approaching German battle cruisers, somehow 'went adrift' in the British communications. At this stage in the proceedings neither side realized that the other's main battle fleet was at sea. Beatty thought that he was about to engage German battle cruisers and hang on to them until Jellicoe came up, while Hipper thought that Scheer's ruse had succeeded and that, while engaging Beatty's forces, he would draw them onwards until Scheer with the High Seas Fleet could destroy him. Both fleets of battle cruisers were now in line ahead on slightly converging courses, their destroyers and light cruisers spread out in advance and to each side of the speeding lines. The sky to the east was now cloudy and hazy, favouring the Germans, while to the west it was still bright, tending to silhouette the British.

The action began between the two ships in the van, Beatty's *Lion* and Hipper's *Lützow,* fire being opened at 3.48 p.m. by *Lion* at 16,500 yards. With her 13.5 inch guns it would have been possible for her to have opened fire earlier, outranging the Germans' 12-inch, but she failed to do so and also failed to get the correct range quickly, while Hipper's ships were soon straddling the British. Their optical instruments, as it was admitted later, were a great deal better, and it is possible also that the constant gunnery training which they had been able to practise unmolested in the Baltic gave them the edge. It is also of course known that their armour-piercing shells with delay fuses were better than the British shells. Three minutes after opening fire *Lion* had been hit twice, so had *Princess Royal* while *Tiger* had received four hits. Hipper had only five battle cruisers to Beatty's six but he soon evened the odds, and it was not until the range was down to under 13,000 yards that the British fire damaged *Seydlitz.* At the rear of the battle line the duel between *Indefatigable* and *Von der Tann* ended abruptly when a salvo from the German hit the British battle cruiser, crashed through her deck, and a magazine went up. She sank after a terrible explosion and only two out of her ship's company of over a thousand were ever recovered.

Throughout the action so far, the handling of the battle cruisers and in particular the communications had been indifferent, and it was only at about this point that the 5th Battle Squadron managed to come up with Beatty's ships, and first discerned through the drifting smoke of action the outlines of the enemy. They opened fire at 19,000 yards, finding the range almost at once and Hipper's battle cruisers ran into a forest of 15-inch shells bursting around them. *Von der Tann* and *Moltke* were both hit and severely damaged, but before they had got into action yet another of Beatty's battle cruisers had gone up in the same way as *Indefatigable* — *Queen Mary,* hit by two salvoes, blowing up as her magazines exploded. Both Beatty and Hipper now sheered away from one another while both sides sent in their destroyers. A confused, fierce small ship action followed, in the course of which *Seydlitz* was severely damaged by a torpedo in the bows. Two destroyers on each side were lost but the damage to *Seydlitz* and the fact that all the German torpedoes had been easily evaded gave some uplift to British morale, somewhat shattered by the fact that they had entered the battle with six battle cruisers to Hipper's five and were now reduced to four, one of those *Lion* herself badly damaged by shell fire.

It was shortly after 4.30 p.m. during this destroyer action that Admiral Beatty's light cruiser squadron, which was four miles ahead of his battle cruisers, saw an awe-inspiring sight. Preceded by light cruisers and headed north towards them the topmasts of a line of great ships were visible. The German High Seas Fleet under Admiral Scheer, confident that the British had taken the bait, was about to spring the trap on the battle cruisers. Commodore Goodenough, in command of the 2nd Light Cruiser Squadron, with his pendant in *Southampton,* sent the urgent signal: 'Have sighted enemy battle fleet, bearing S.E. Enemy's course north.' He then gave his own position and, acting in proper fashion for the nature of his command, pressed on towards the enemy, knowing that his commander-in-chief would want to know the size and composition of the force.

Realizing his dangerous position Beatty ordered a reversal of course 180 degrees, heading back for the Grand Fleet, which was still out of sight over the horizon. Admiral Hipper, fulfilling his function of holding on to the British battle cruisers, turned to follow. Meanwhile Goodenough with the 2nd Light Cruiser Squadron held on towards the enemy, until he was clearly able to make out at least sixteen or seventeen great ships coming towards him in line ahead. In the misty failing light the Germans probably mistook them for some of Hipper's own light cruisers and it was not until, with the range down to 13,000 yards, Goodenough swung his ships round to head back north that they were easily recognized by their silhouettes, and the leading German ships opened up on them. He managed to escape without any serious damage to his cruiser squadron and send the amplifying report that the German High Seas Fleet was at sea and headed north.

Admiral Scheer felt confident that his plan had worked, that he had managed to trap the British battle cruisers and would soon destroy them. He had been disconcerted when he had heard of the presence of the squadron of battleships as well, but concluded all the same that he had run into only a slightly more sizeable part of the British fleet, and that he would easily be able to destroy this even bigger prey with the weight of ships he had with him.

In the confusion of the action, coupled with the sudden reversal of course, it seems as if the signal had never been made for the British battleships astern of Beatty's battle cruisers to do the same. Now, as Beatty's ships flashed past, they received the signal to alter course 180 degrees after him in succession. The right signal would have been for them to alter course together, but the manoeuvre ordered meant that, as they altered round one after another, the leading ships of the German High Seas Fleet were able to bring a concentrated fire to bear on them. Two were fairly heavily hit, *Barham* and *Malaya*, but neither so badly as to be forced out of the line, while they in their turn scored hits on two of the leading German battleships. As they formed up in line ahead and headed north after Beatty they in their turn swept past the German battle cruisers, scoring hits on *Lützow* and *Derfflinger* and causing heavy damage to the already-torpedoed *Seydlitz*. It is a tribute to the German construction methods of torpedo bulkheads and honeycomb compartments that this battle cruiser still stayed afloat and in the line, whereas had she been British she would probably have been compelled to drop out, or possibly have sunk.

Jellicoe's Grand Fleet was drawing southward still in its compact cruising order at twenty knots, and still ignorant — so poor were communications — that the German High Seas Fleet was so close astern of Beatty and his ships. Admiral Scheer, for his part, was still completely unaware that the Grand Fleet was at sea, and having the squadron of British battleships and their battle cruisers retreating before Hipper, assumed that he was closing in for the planned kill and signalled the 'general chase'.

Scheer's speed was limited by the fact that he had with him a number of the older German battleships, but even so the two huge fleets were almost blindly running upon one another at a combined speed of 35 knots or more. Scheer, having had no reports from the submarines that had been detailed in advance to watch Scapa Flow, had no idea that a general engagement was at hand.

Admiral Hood with three battle cruisers had been sent ahead of the Grand Fleet to cut off those with which Beatty had been engaged from any escape route through the Skagerrak, while Admiral Jellicoe remained unaware through errors in navigational positions (both aboard his own flagship, *Iron Duke,* and Beatty's *Lion*) just how close was the High Seas Fleet. It was not until 6.14 p.m. when *Lion* dashed across to take up her station ahead of Jellicoe's leading battleships that the disconcerting message was flashed to the flagship that the German battle fleet was in sight to the south west. The Grand Fleet was deployed only just in time from its cruising formation into line on the port column. This was admirably executed and twenty minutes later, when the twenty-four battleships were in line ahead, they were turned more southerly from the course which they had been steering so as to bring them onto the given line of bearing of the enemy.

The battle cruisers under Admiral Hood had now got into action, disabling the cruiser *Wiesbaden.* It was at about this time that Admiral Scheer suddenly and devastatingly

became aware what was happening, when Rear Admiral
Behncke, who was in the van aboard *König*, saw in the
distance ahead of him a long and seemingly endless line of
great grey ships curving across the horizon and crossing his
'T'. From a 'general chase' after British battle cruisers and
a squadron of battleships, which had fallen into a carefully
prepared trap, the Germans realized that they had fallen
into a greater one themselves. It must at once be said that,
while this was something which Jellicoe had long planned
and hoped for, the British admiral had been almost equally
surprised by the speed with which it had occurred.

Hipper's already damaged battle cruisers ahead of the
High Seas Fleet now came under a rain of fire, as did the
leading ships of the van. At the same time those outriders
of the fleets, destroyers and light cruisers, were already
in action against one another while the light cruiser
Wiesbaden which had been lying stopped and disabled from
the fire of Hood's ships proved too great a lure for Admiral
Arbuthnot, leading the 1st Heavy Cruiser Squadron in
Defence, who dashed up to give her the *coup-de-grâce*. The
apparent almost indestructibility of German-built ships
was demonstrated by the fact that *Wiesbaden* did not sink
despite the battering she received, and while Arbuthnot's
cruisers were so engaged they themselves suffered disaster.
The 3rd Squadron of German battleships at the head of
their line suddenly loomed through the mist and smoke and,
finding no larger target, opened fire on the British cruisers.
Arbuthnot's flagship, severely hit, caught on fire and her
ammunition blew up. She left no more than a cloud of smoke
over the scene, while *Warrior*, severely damaged and on fire,
just managed to turn away and come under the protection
of the 5th Battle Squadron. *Black Prince*, shot through and
through, fell astern of the fleet and became as forgotten as if
she had been sunk. At the same moment as *Warrior* closed
the 5th Battle Squadron the helm of *Warspite* jammed to
starboard and nothing that could be done by using her
engines could counteract it. She swerved round in full sight
of the German van and was hit several times by heavy shells.

She was gradually brought under some kind of control, but was still to all intents and purposes unmanageable and forced to retire from action. She was later taken in tow by the seaplane carrier *Engadine*. Admiral Hood's battle cruisers throughout this phase were pouring their fire upon Hipper's battle cruisers, already damaged from their previous engagements with Beatty's squadron, and only their fine construction saved them from the destruction that was soon to overtake Hood himself. Hipper's *Lützow,* badly damaged though she was, continued engaging *Invincible* while at the same time Behncke's battleship *König* in the van of the advancing line of the High Seas Fleet opened fire on her. The effect was devastating as one salvo or more plunged down on her and she was torn apart by the terrible explosion of her magazines.

The smoke of the battle had been spread like a grey curtain over the sea so that the main fleets had been invisible to one another but now, as Scheer recounted in his Memoirs, he himself suddenly saw ahead of him the line of great ships, miles long, each end of it disappearing into the mist. At the same moment, all along that line to the north, came the blaze of guns and a rain of shells began to fall on the ships in the German van. It had never been Scheer's intention to challenge the Grand Fleet itself, and he realized that his ships were pressing on to destruction, with the enemy like a net folding around them. Such a situation had been allowed for in many thorough tactical exercises. At 6.35 p.m. he made the signal for all ships to turn 180 degrees to starboard and, as the battleships began to turn in retreat, destroyers raced forward to cover the operation, laying a heavy smoke screen between them and the enemy. Nothing could now be seen by Jellicoe's ships except the great bank of smoke lying ahead and merging into the cloud and mist that already obscured the sea. Hipper's battle cruisers also executed the turn, astern of the main fleet, but his flagship *Lützow,* afire and badly crippled, could not keep up with them and limped away almost sinking to the south west through the sheltering smoke.

As a great silence fell across the sea that a few minutes before had been ear-splitting with gunfire and thunderous with the explosions of battle, both sides were afforded a brief respite to take stock of the position. Scheer knew that he could not hold his present course for long since he was steaming away from the Jade, his source of safety, for his only hope was to escape. Jellicoe on the other hand held on steadily southwards, supposing the German fleet to be headed south west and hoping to lay himself between them and the minefields of the Heligoland Bight. Although he could not know it Jellicoe's great chance was gone, and indeed his supreme achievement in laying the Grand Fleet so perfectly across the High Seas Fleet would be dissipated within the following hours. He was badly served by his scouting forces, and the cruisers which should have been bringing him information seem to have to made too little attempt to press on through the obscurity and keep him in touch with the fleeing enemy. Poor signalling and communications generally were shown to be the greatest weaknesses of the British throughout the whole operation.

Scheer, assuming that the Grand Fleet was in pursuit, decided on a second reversal of course, this time to eastwards in the hope of passing astern of it and thus making for the most northerly of the channels through the German minefields and reaching the safety of the Jade and Wilhelmshaven. In doing so he ran into the tail end of the Grand Fleet and was forced into yet another battle turn away. To cover this further retreat he sent ahead his already battered battle cruisers, followed by torpedo boats, in a heroic last attempt to confuse and break up if possible the enemy's line. In this he was successful beyond any of his expectations, for he had quite unwittingly hit upon Jellicoe's Achilles heel. The British admiral, himself a gunnery specialist, had an almost inordinate fear of the possibilities of mass torpedo attacks on a line of battleships. In the Grand Fleet Battle Orders he had laid down: 'Until the enemy is beaten by gunfire, it is not my intention to risk attack from his torpedoes...it is to be understood that my intention is to keep outside torpedo range of the enemy's battle line.' The words 'generally speaking' were placed before the last sentence, and this was certainly a situation in which the fleet should have been turned towards the enemy's attack, since it was the latter who was trying to escape. It is always easy to be wise after the event (and Jutland was to provoke countless books and never-ending arguments over the coming years), but it was at this moment, when signalling the turn away, that Jellicoe lost the chance of bringing to a triumphant conclusion the battle for which he had so long prepared. In the event, many torpedoes were fired and not a single hit was scored, thus confirming a lesson that might have been learned from the Far East — the erratic nature and uncertainty of torpedo boat attacks. The German battle cruisers having completed their diversion, and several torpedo boats having been lost in the immense weight of fire poured upon them from the secondary armament of the British battleships, disappeared behind smoke and the darkening mist. At this moment both fleets were steaming away from one another and Scheer's High Seas Fleet vanished from sight.

The opportunity of Jutland was lost and, in the real sense, the battle was over. By the time that Jellicoe had come about and resumed his southerly course any chance of a major engagement being resumed, and the well-laid trap finally sprung, had gone. Jellicoe's assumption, based on conflicting reports and misleading information, was wrong. Scheer had resumed his course to the south east and, about an hour before midnight, the main body of the German Fleet passed astern of the Grand Fleet, headed for safety. Its passage did not remain undetected by the screens of light craft in the rear of the British fleet and occasioned a series of desperate and hastily undertaken attacks by destroyers which suddenly found themselves in the middle of the German fleet. Several British destroyers were lost in the course of these, but they registered the only successful torpedo attacks of the day — sinking the light cruiser *Rostock* and the old battleship *Pommern*. The unfortunate cruiser *Black Prince*, lying disabled in their path, was raked by ship after ship of the German line and blew up with all hands.

The flashes from these night encounters were clearly seen from the rear of Jellicoe's main fleet but, amazing though it seems, the information never seems to have reached the admiral that enemy heavy ships were passing astern of his course. Enemy destroyer attacks had certainly been expected, and it seems to have been assumed that no more than this was happening. It remains somewhat astonishing that Jellicoe and his staff should have made no inquiry as to the cause of the disturbances in the rear. Still confident of sighting the enemy at dawn, the Grand Fleet steamed onwards in the wrong direction. By 3 a.m., while the British were anxiously scanning the horizon, Scheer had the Horns Reef lightship abeam and the High Seas Fleet was as good as home. Overnight, apart from the two sinkings in British destroyer attacks, he had lost one light cruiser through collision with a battleship, and had been forced to sink Hipper's *Lützow* by torpedo, after taking off all her crew. He could congratulate himself on a lucky escape, not even knowing that by almost a miracle his fleet had passed through a gap in a minefield laid a few hours before by the minelayer *Abdiel* on Jellicoe's orders.

Jutland was the anticlimax to decades of the exaltation of the great iron-clad capital ship. The immensely high hopes of the British public were brought low, while the Germans could congratulate themselves on having faced a superior force, inflicted considerable damage, and extricated themselves from a deadly trap with great skill. Not surprisingly, it was hailed in Germany as a victory. For the loss of one old battleship, one battle cruiser, and four light cruisers, they had sunk three battle cruisers and three armoured cruisers. Both sides also had a number of destroyer losses, although the British had lost more through their night attacks when surprised by the passage of the German fleet. Unknown of course at the time was the amount of serious damage incurred by either side. Subsequent accounts would reveal that, apart from destroyers, seven major British ships required extensive repairs while, on the other hand, seventeen of their German equivalents were in dockyard hands for many months. The British losses in officers and men, however, were double the German, largely through the losses of their battle cruisers.

A German naval expert recognized that '...on 1 June 1916, it was clear to every thinking person that this battle must, and would be, the last one.' This was certainly understood by Admiral Scheer, who realized that the High Seas Fleet had come near the edge of disaster by exposing itself to a situation for which it was never intended. Soon he was informing the Kaiser of his opinion. He stated clearly that victory on the High Seas lay not with capital ships and surface warfare, but with that new arm which Germany had developed to its peak — the U-boat and submarine warfare against an island that depended on its trade routes.

The arguments that raged in Britain, and persisted for decades on the subject of Jutland, are far removed now, not only by the years but by the intervention of a World War II. The pro-Beatty or Jellicoe schools are meaningless except to the historian, but one thing remains clear — 'Jellicoe was the only man who could have lost the war in an afternoon.' Excessively cautious he may have been, but he bore that immense responsibility. Beatty, on the other hand, was largely to blame for the poor use of the new *Queen Elizabeth* class (the four fastest and best battleships on either side) in the opening stages of the battle, while his superior, Jellicoe, was equally at fault in the later phases. Only one thing was very evident: the inadequate horizontal armouring of the battle cruisers against descending shells was the cause of their traumatic losses. As Fisher had previously remarked: 'No one can know the results of such a battle until it comes.'

On the technical side the Germans were shown to have better optical equipment for their range finders, and their armour-piercing shells were deadly while the British shells were indifferent, often exploding on impact — something quite useless against heavily armoured vessels. In their ability to endure more damage without either sinking or blowing up the German construction was shown as far sounder but, as has been said, was suitable only for their one task which was more or less confined to action in the North Sea. British designers and constructors could not be blamed for the fact that their ships had to be able to operate anywhere in the world, far from home bases and barracks for their men. The protection of the magazines was something that occupied immediate attention, the British having learned by bitter experience at Jutland what the Germans had learned the same hard way earlier. The protection of the vitals of big ships by adequate horizontal armour against dropping shells was still not given sufficient attention and a giant among ships, laid down before the end of the war, was to suffer for this and in due course was to die like Beatty's three battle cruisers for the same reason in World War II.

Jutland was the battle that nobody won. But in long terms, the fact that the High Seas Fleet never ventured out again in force was conclusive. It was certainly the greatest, and equally the last, major battle in which the great warship — in the form by which it had hitherto been known — would predominate.

CHAPTER ELEVEN

Sunset Years

It was among the German High Seas fleet, grown sullen during the years that they had become captives within German harbours, that the mutiny had festered which contributed to the collapse of their country in 1918. Surrendered in the November of that year, the great ships which had proved themselves in every way the equals of their British enemy on their one encounter were interned in Scapa Flow under the guns of the Royal Navy. Britain's allies, unwilling that her navy should benefit to such an immense extent as adding the German fleet to her own, were adamant that, until their fate had been decided upon, they should remain in the custody of their interned German crews. The solution to this rankling problem was presented on 21 June 1919 when, with the exception of one battleship and five light cruisers, the whole High Seas fleet — with all its great battleships and battle cruisers — was scuttled by its own crews. Thus, in a gesture that was almost symbolic of the fate of the capital ship, the last of the German Imperial Navy went down in the grey waters of the north.

Although throughout the inter-war years all major industrialized countries continued in varying degrees to build new battleships, even the most conservative conceded in their hearts that Jutland had shown that the battleship was no longer the winner of great victories. The vessel that would dominate World War II, particularly in the Pacific, was the aircraft carrier, in which Britain had been the first navy to take an active interest. But so long as the uneasy years of peace prevailed there still remained the necessity for countries to demonstrate their power and importance by the display of their flag at various places throughout the world. This was especially true of all countries with colonial empires, and true also of those countries like the United States and Japan which sought to exercise spheres of influence outside of their own territories. For Britain above all, with its great empire stretching from the West Indies to India and the Far East, the guarding presence of the mother country needed to be displayed, and nothing had yet arisen more suitable than the great capital ship.

There was always also the need to keep a powerful naval force in areas where foreign countries were displaying warlike intentions, especially if these in any way might affect the British lifeline to India and the Far East. The instability of the countries surrounding the Mediterranean basin made this area particularly important largely on account of the Suez Canal. With the rise of Mussolini and the fascists in Italy and their increasing interest in African colonies, the British Mediterranean fleet with its main base in the island of Malta became one of the most important naval appointments, something that was to be made even clearer by the Abyssinian war and, later, the Spanish Civil War. One of the battleships which, in company with her sister ships, had been launched in World War I (and was to go on to serve with great distinction in World War II) was HMS *Warspite*. This *Queen Elizabeth* class ship, as has been said, was the finest class of battleships that ever saw active service in any navy in the period before all such great armoured warships became extinct. During the interwar years, with fairly regular refits to keep them updated, they served Britain well not only by 'showing the flag' in foreign countries or in British colonies and dominions, but also by their powerful presence at varying times throughout troubled areas of the world. Before World War II broke out, *Warspite* and three of her sister ships had been almost completely reconstructed — new engines, new boilers, the addition of further deck armour, anti-aircraft batteries, anti-torpedo bulges and so on — thus making them almost new ships. In those years of great financial strain the cost of designing and building a complete new class of battleships had thus been obviated.

One of the most famous ships during this period, known throughout many countries in the world because of her almost constant processions to parts of the British Empire, was the largest ship in the world, HMS *Hood*. She had been laid down in 1916 following information that the Germans were building a battle cruiser with 15-inch guns. Launched only three months before the surrender of the German fleet, *Hood* was the most expensive ship to be built in her time, and in every respect the largest warship afloat for many years to come. Eight hundred and sixty feet long, by 104 feet wide, with a draught of 28.5 feet, she displaced 41,200 tons, and had a speed of 32 knots. Her main armament consisted of eight 15-inch guns in their twin turrets fore and aft, with a secondary armament of twelve 5.5 inch guns, while anti-aircraft guns were added later. The lessons of Jutland had been but partly absorbed and although her side armour had been increased from 9 to 12 inches, her deck armour still remained relatively weak, and it was the effect of plunging fire on the battle cruisers which had been the principal cause of the losses at Jutland. Her name came from a family of great sailors, most distinguished among them being Viscount Samuel Hood renowned for his brilliant actions against the French in the West Indies during the late eighteenth century. A lineal descendant of his had been Rear-Admiral Hood who had died in the battle cruiser *Invincible* at Jutland. An eye-witness account of how he met his end was uncannily prophetic of the death in 1941 of the ship that bore his name.

Hood pressed home his attack, and it was an inspiring sight to see this squadron of battle cruisers dashing towards the enemy with every gun in action. On the *Lion's* bridge we felt like cheering them on, for it seemed that the decisive moment of the battle had come. Our feelings, however, suffered a sudden change, for just when success was in our grasp, the *Invincible* was hit by a salvo amidships. Several big explosions followed, great tongues of flame shot out from her riven side, the masts collapsed, the ship broke in two, and an enormous pall of black smoke rose to the sky. One moment she was the proud flagship full of life, intent on her prey; the next, she was just two sections of twisted metal, the bow and the stern standing up out of the water like two large tombstones suddenly raised in honour of a thousand and twenty-six British dead; an astonishing sight, probably unique in naval warfare.

*Hood*s world cruise starting in November 1923 now seems like an image of a very remote world, but it is worth considering, however briefly, since it was so typical of other 'flag-showing' cruises made by the great ships of the great Powers for a century prior to World War I and in the subsequent uneasy years between the wars. (More recently somewhat similar displays of power are still made by the nuclear giants, but they are kept at low key for they are no longer particularly welcomed by the other nations.) Welcome was certainly extended to *Hood* and her ship's company as leader of the special squadron sent on this world cruise taking eleven months. With her went *Repulse*, an earlier and conventional battle cruiser (destined to be sunk by Japanese air attack in 1941), and the 1st Light Cruiser Squadron, consisting of *Delhi, Dauntless, Dragon* and *Dunedin*. They pursued the now vanished path of Empire via Freetown in West Africa, Cape Town and other South African ports, Zanzibar, Ceylon and Singapore to Australia. Hundreds of thousands of people visited *Hood* and the other ships in the squadron in Australia and Tasmania. That such cruises did indeed serve the purpose for which they were largely intended is confirmed by an editorial in the Melbourne *Sun* at the time: 'To say that Australia was cradled in the strong arms of the British Navy is more than a figure of speech. It was the command of the seas that made a British Australia possible. It is due to British sea power that Australia is the only continent that has never had to suffer an invasion....'

From New Zealand, where the reception was equal to that in Australia (78,000 people visited *Hood* in Wellington), the squadron sailed on across the Pacific to the Fiji Islands, a British colony, and then via other British island colonies to American Honolulu, and to Canada, where between Victoria and Vancouver nearly a quarter of a million visitors came aboard the ships. On her way south for her passage through the Panama Canal *Hood* and the squadron called at San Francisco, to receive a welcome that would hardly have been extended to a visiting sovereign or head of state. A reporter on the *New York Herald Tribune* sheds a revealing light on the puritan conscience of America at that time:

> In a blare of whistles and saluting cannon seven men of war steam through the Golden Gate and come to anchor in San Francisco Harbour. The Admiral, in a profound deference to the inexplicable peculiarity of our institutions commands that no rum is to be served out during the three days of the visit [the wardroom bars were also closed]; and one senses the magnificence of the gesture, for his flag is hoisted in HMS *Hood* the most powerful ship of the British Navy. San Francisco reports that this is the most important British squadron to anchor in an American harbour for forty years....

A closing sidelight on the difficulties that the sheer size of *Hood* occasioned is revealed by The Panama Canal Record for the year. *Hood* and *Repulse* were the two largest vessels ever to use the waterway up to that date, the main difficulty being occasioned by *Hood's* beam for the width of the lock chambers was then only 110 feet, thus giving a clearance of only two and a half feet on either side of the warship, while her underwater anti-torpedo bulges added a further problem. There was not much clearance at the bows and stern either, about 70 foot fore and aft, since the usable length of the locks was 1000 feet. The battle cruiser's displacement at the time of her passage was 44,799 tons. The fact that *Hood* remained throughout her life officially the largest capital ship afloat was due to the Washington Conference of 1921, when Great Britain, France, Italy and Japan, at the invitation of President Harding of the United States, sent their respective delegates to confer on the limitation of national amaments. In those days, particularly in America, a heady air blew from distant Geneva and the aspirations of the peacelovers were able to override any bounds of actuality. The American Secretary of State immediately proposed that, 'for a period of not less than 10 years there shall be no further construction of capital ships'. This was something that at the time Britain was prepared to accept, since cruisers were regarded as the lifeline of the Empire, and they faced no immediate challenge in the European sphere to their present dominant position. At that date, of course, it could in no way be foreseen how close was the time when the age of the dictators would begin, or that Germany — not even considered at the Washington Conference — would start rebuilding her navy. Under Hitler the published figures for her new ships such as pocket battleships, and even full-sized battleships like *Bismarck* and *Tirpitz*, would bear no relation to the truth.

In December 1921 agreement, was reached in Washington that the United States and Great Britain should maintain naval parity with 525,000 tons of capital ships each; Japan should have 315,000 tons and Italy and France 175,000 tons each. The Japanese had fought hard to secure their additional tonnage, which was accepted by Britain only on the condition that she should be allowed to build two new battleships of not more than 35,000 tons apiece, while the United States should complete two new ships that were already in the process of construction. The two new British ships, *Nelson* and *Rodney,* built under the restrictions that battleships were not to be more than 35,000 tons, became known as the 'Washington Ships' because of their truncated appearance resulting from this treaty. Because the Japanese at the time were already building two battleships with 16-inch guns, this calibre was made the general rule instead of 15-inch. The result was that both *Nelson* and *Rodney* were armed with nine 16-inch guns mounted in three triple turrets forward. The two ships were 710 feet long on a beam of 106 feet with a draught of 30 feet. Their armour was 14 inches thick and their speed 23 knots. To conform to the rule, their displacement was 33,950 tons, but actually 38,000 tons when fully loaded. A further consequence of the Washington Treaty was the so-called 'Ten Year Rule' which was a formula for governments based on the assumption that there would be no major war for at least ten years. This led to a decline on naval spending in Britain and, by the time that the turn of events in Europe had become clear even to the most pacifically minded, the new Germany of Adolf Hitler and the fascist Italy of Mussolini were firmly established.

In 1929, for instance, the keel of the 'pocket batleship' *Deutschland* was laid, to be followed by *Admiral Scheer* and *Admiral Graf Spee*. Faster than any battleships existing at the time, though not as fast as the battle cruiser *Hood*, their diesel engines gave them a great range and their 11-inch guns made them more heavily armed than any cruisers. Soon, throwing aside any pretence at keeping within the boundaries of any treaties (especially that of Versailles), in 1934 Hitler approved the construction of the battleships *Scharnhorst* and *Gneisenau* of 31,300 tons. These were to be followed in 1939 by the launchings of *Bismarck* and *Tirpitz*, officially 35,000 tons, but with a design displacement of 45,000 and when fully loaded actually displacing 52,600 tons. With a speed of over 30 knots and a main armament of eight 15-inch guns, they were undoubtedly at the time the largest capital ships in the world. Once World War II had started, even they would be outclassed by the Japanese giants, *Yamato* and *Musashi*. Even the great American *Iowa* class of battleships, laid down in 1940, although slightly longer, narrower and faster, did not quite attain to the power of *Yamato*. She was 862.5 feet in length, 128 feet on the beam, with a draught of 35 feet, and displacing at full load 70,321 tons. Armed with nine 18-inch guns (the largest ever to be mounted on a ship) and literally hundreds of other guns ranging from 6-inch to small calibre light anti-aircraft guns, she carried seven aircraft which were launched by catapults, and was capable of 27.7 knots. The political aim of these giants was to be so formidable in all respects that even the industrially and economically superior USA would be hard pressed to come up with anything to rival them in the near future, and indeed they could not be built on the American east coast since they would be unable to pass through the Panama Canal. Neither they nor the great American battleships were ever to engage in any kind of surface action even remotely resembling Jutland for, as a new type of war evolved in the Pacific area, the giant that now wielded power was the aircraft carrier. Battleships in the Pacific were used in their old secondary role of bombarding enemy-held positions, troop concentrations, and fortified areas. They were also of necessity used as convoy escorts just in case the enemy should deploy a battleship as a convoy raider.

The strong criticism that had been directed against capital ships in the 1920s was understandable in view of the period, but the fact remained that a capital ship was no more than the largest unit of a fleet, and so long as other countries possessed them Britain, dependent on its overseas communications, had to have them as well. So, while ships like *Warspite* of the old navy were constantly refitted and updated, *Nelson* and *Rodney* were built in the 1920s. It was not until 1937, however, that the new class of *King George V* battleships were laid down. Ten 14-inch guns formed the main armament, four of them in each of two turrets fore and aft, and two in a turret superposed forward. As with all capital ships designed for World War II great attention was given to anti-aircraft armament, sixteen 5.25 inch high level guns, similar to those fitted to the navy's new light cruisers, and sixty 2-pr. A.A. guns as well as many Bofors and Oerlikons.

Britain's major contribution during this period was made by her scientists, who had developed the Asdic (Sonar) system for underwater detection to a higher degree than any other country, and this was to prove all-important in the battle against the U-boat in World War II. The other major British invention was RDF, 'radio direction finding' (Radar), which, while first conceived as a warning system against aircraft, was quickly transferred to ships for aircraft detection and ship detection. Another refinement was its use for gunnery ranging, so that a ship having been detected by night or by day with the general 'sweep' radar could then be locked onto by the gunnery radar and its range very precisely determined.

There were to be no further actions in the North Sea even remotely resembling the battle-cruiser engagements of World War I let alone the fumbled encounter of giants at Jutland. The large German surface ships were few in number and intended for no more than lightning descents upon convoys in the Atlantic, followed by a swift return through the dark northern approaches between the ocean and the North Sea. Late in 1940 the pocket battleship *Admiral Scheer,* for instance, successfully broke out into the Atlantic and sank a number of British merchant ships, and would have sunk more but for the suicidal bravery of the armed merchant cruiser *Jervis Bay* in defence of her convoy. In the spring of 1941, at a time when everything was at its darkest for Britain and it was clear that the real battle of the Atlantic had begun, with Germany master of Europe and only the convoy-dependent British Isles holding out, the German operation *Rheinuebung* was set in motion. Originally intended for April it was delayed for some weeks because one of the two ships involved, the heavy cruiser *Prinz Eugen,* had been damaged by a mine. Once this was repaired, she in company with the great battleship *Bismarck* were to set out. With complete disregard for the Washington Treaty *Prinz Eugen* displaced 14,500 tons, while the British 'County Class' cruisers only displaced their regulated 10,000. She mounted a main armament of eight 8-inch, twelve 4.1 inch, and thirty-eight light anti-aircraft guns as well as carrying twelve torpedo tubes. With this armament and her maximum speed of 33 knots she had achieved what in earlier days American ships like *Old Ironsides* had also been designed for — an ability to outrun battleships and at the same time to out-gun other ships theoretically of her own class. Again, like *Bismarck* herself, she was subdivided into more watertight compartments than any comparable British ship, and at her economical cruising speed of 20 knots had a 10,000 mile radius of action.

Operation *Rheinuebung* planned for *Bismarck* accompanied by the *Prinz Eugen*, both of which had done many exercises in preparation together in the Baltic, to pass through the Denmark Strait between Iceland and Greenland into the Atlantic and fall upon the convoys there. At this time of year in the strait the Greenland ice pack would only have left about sixty miles of navigable sea and the weather conditions were likely to be such that British air and sea patrols would be reduced. With the aim of deluding the British into thinking that, if a breakout was indeed intended, it was through one of the more southern routes between Scotland and Greenland, the two ships made their point of departure Bergen in Norway, which was known to come within regular British air surveillance. On 21 May they were indeed seen there, and correctly identified by a British reconnaisance aircraft and the assumption might well have been made that Bergen was an unlikely point of departure for the Denmark Strait. It suggested that one of the other four more southern channels might be intended. While holding back the main body of the fleet until further information came through, the commander-in-chief, Admiral Tovey, ordered the County Class cruiser *Suffolk*, which was refuelling in Iceland, to rejoin her sister ship *Norfolk*, already on patrol in the Denmark Strait. Weather conditions had been steadily worsening over the whole area and while he could quite quickly cover the more southern aproaches to the Atlantic from his fleet base, he was concerned about the most northern of all, the most unlikely perhaps from the last known position of *Bismarck* and *Prinz Eugen,* and yet for this and other reasons the most likely of all. In advance of the planned break out of *Bismarck* and *Prinz Eugen* the Germans had sailed five oil tankers and two supply ships carrying ammunition and victuals into the Atlantic to take up appointed stations over an area ranging from the coast of Greenland to the South Atlantic. If all went well for the raiders, these would enable them to prolong their *guerre de course*. Vice-Admiral Lutjens, with his flag in *Bismarck,* was in command of the operation when in the dark hours and poor weather of 21 May they slipped from Bergen and headed north. Just two hours later, at midnight from Scapa Flow, the two capital ships chosen by the commander-in-chief to watch the Denmark Strait also got under way. They were *Hood* and *Prince of Wales.*

Admiral Tovey had had at his disposal an inadequate fleet to cover the various escape routes which covered thousands of square miles — *Hood, Prince of Wales,* his own flagship, *King George V,* and the old battle cruiser *Repulse. Hood* was old but better armed than *Repulse,* although that major defect of the inadequacy of her deck armour had never, for one reason and another, been remedied throughout all the previous years of uneasy peace when she had been hastening from one trouble spot to another. *Prince of Wales,* on the other hand, had only joined the fleet a few weeks before, her crew and the new ship herself were not even 'worked up', and her 14-inch turrets were of a new type and still suffering from numerous teething troubles. It was only on paper that they might have looked more than a match for the German battleship and heavy cruiser. Accompanied by six destroyers, they now sailed to Iceland, there to refuel and hold themselves in readiness.

The new aircraft carrier *Victorious* was also put at the disposal of the commander-in-chief, but she suffered from much the same defects as *Prince of Wales,* being newly commissioned and just diverted from a Gibraltar convoy which would have been her first real operation. An air reconnaisance report that the battleship and cruiser had left Bergen served to bring the whole British fleet to action stations. While the commander-in-chief ordered his ships in company to prepare for sea, *Hood* and *Prince of Wales* were diverted from Iceland to take up patrol to the south west of the great island, so as to be on hand if the enemy should come through the Iceland-Faeroes passage or the northerly Denmark Strait. The commander-in-chief and the ships with him were heading northwards to close the gap between the Orkneys and the patrol line on which *Hood* and *Prince of Wales* were operating. The weather in the Denmark Strait was so thick that visibility was down to a hundred yards, and into this the German admiral was comfortably sliding, confident that no British air patrols — even if flown at all — could see his two ships, and trusting that they had no sea patrols in the strait and had been misled by his feint of leaving from Bergen.

Suffolk and the *Norfolk* were in fact covering the area through which *Bismarck* and *Prinz Eugen* were now advancing, but it was a wide enough front to keep a watch upon and both the cruisers, while fitted with early radar, did not yet have the new type that could rotate through 360 degrees. It was at 7.22 p.m. in the northern twilight that the two great enemy ships were sighted together by a lookout in *Suffolk*, less than 14,000 yards away. *Suffolk's* helm was put hard down and she slid into the mist that lay to port of her, before she herself had been seen by the enemy. The Germans were steering 240 degrees at high speed, 28 to 30 knots, and it would be all that the two British cruisers could do to hang on to them through the Arctic night. About 300 miles away Admiral Holland in *Hood* got the sighting report. He and his force altered course to intercept, while about 600 miles to the south east the commander-in-chief in *King George V* made an alteration of course so that, if the enemy turned south to elude Admiral Holland, they would find him waiting for them. Admiral Lutjens did not know that he had been detected and that the enemy was already preparing to intercept him, until suddenly, at 8.30 p.m., *Norfolk* accidentally burst out of a blanket of mist at full speed. Even as she turned away the first of a series of three 15-inch salvoes fell around her. The German shooting now as later was admirable, flying splinters of giant shells bursting aboard as *Norfolk* snaked away at full speed, laying a wreath of concealing smoke behind her.

At that time of the year the Arctic twilight hardly ever descends to complete darkness and in this eerie greyness pursuers and pursued tore through the icy Denmark Strait. Only one British cruiser had been sighted, and Admiral Lutjens decided to take the risk of pressing on into the Atlantic rather than abandon his mission at this early stage. The British might have no capital ships within easy call, and if his two ships could shake off the cruiser they still might well be off and away into the vastness of the Atlantic before full daylight. Snow flurries, rain storms and mist patches also confused the night, and if it had not been for their radar the cruisers might indeed have lost track of the enemy. This, in fact, they were to do during a period when *Bismarck* had disappeared into a snow storm. *Suffolk,* the only cruiser at that moment in radar contact, lost her in the 'clutter' on her radar scan caused by the snow, in which she herself was also engulfed. It was not until 2.47 a.m. that she was found again and from now on nothing could stop the final encounter.

As full daylight dawned Admiral Lutjens may well have felt that, even if the British cruiser that had been engaged was still in contact with him, he and his ships were almost out of the narrow and dangerous strait and before many hours might be well away. At 5.30 a.m. however, he sighted smoke to the south; it was from *Hood* and *Prince of Wales,* rushing at full speed to intercept him. They were still over the horizon and there could be no way of knowing what ships they were. Action stations sounded in *Bismarck* and *Prinz Eugen* at almost the same minute as in *Hood* and *Prince of Wales.*

Space does not permit an analysis of the action, and all that can be said is that it was brief but terrible — and a credit to the German gunnery. At 5.52 a.m. when the range had come down to 25,000 yards, *Hood* in the van was the first to open fire. She was followed within seconds by *Bismarck* and *Prince of Wales* which was following *Hood* at a distance of 800 yards (close order formation). Misled by the resemblance between the silhouettes of the two German ships, *Hood* had fired first at the *Prinz Eugen* which was the leading ship. *Bismarck's* first salvo fell ahead of *Hood* and her second astern, while watchers in *Norfolk* and *Suffolk* thought that *Hoods* second salvo (she had shifted target from *Prinz Eugen* on the mistake being realized) fell near the German battleship, while her third seemed to straddle her. *Bismarck's* third salvo appeared to score a hit on *Hood,* causing an upper deck fire.

The two British ships which had opened fire on a closing course were now turning, one behind the other, so as to open their 'A' arcs and allow the full weight of their salvoes to be brought to bear. Salvoes from both sides were in the air when with her fifth *Bismarck* gave *Hood* her death blow. The great battle cruiser died almost exactly as *Invincible* had at Jutland with Rear-Admiral Hood aboard. Guns and turrets were hurled aloft like toys, her back broke, and out of the great flame and smoke of the explosion her bows and stern lifted momentarily like tombstones. *Prince of Wales* following so close astern of her was forced to alter course to avoid the wreckage.

The untried and untested *Prince of Wales* (one of her forward turrets had become defective after the first salvo) now suffered a hit that wrecked her bridge and caused bad damage aft. At almost the same time she had scored three hits on *Bismarck*. These were to lead Admiral Lutjens to the conclusion that operation *Rheinuebung* was effectively cancelled. The great German battleship had one boiler room flooded and her speed accordingly reduced, and a hit in her port oil bunker had contaminated her fuel-supply system as well as causing a serious loss of fuel. Amid driving rain squalls that reduced visibility practically to zero, the action between the great ships now came to an end.

The badly damaged *Prince of Wales* remained with the shadowing cruisers, Admiral Lutjens managed to detach *Prinz Eugen* to make her escape during the blinding weather, while *Bismarck* endeavoured to make her way to Brest for repairs. The rest of this classic drama of the hounding down of *Bismarck* is well enough known. Assailed by battleships, carrier-borne torpedo aircraft, cruisers and destroyers, she finally sank not far from the aircover that would have been afforded out of Brest. She had been fought gallantly to the very last and only 115 survivors were picked up out of all her crew. From *Hood* there were three.

Bismarck had proved not only the quality of German naval gunnery (evidenced in World War I), but that German construction, within its specialized limits, could produce ships that were almost impossible to sink. That there were no 'unsinkable ships' was later to be demonstrated far away in the Pacific. (Seamen have always known that this term was fabricated for the reassurance of landsmen.) It had indeed been used about *Bismarck*, and it had also been used about the gigantic *Yamato* and *Musashi*. Both were finally sunk by American planes — forty direct bomb hits and eighteen torpedo hits accounting for the latter in the Gulf of Leyte in 1944, and almost as many for *Yamato* in the final stages of the Far East war. By the end of World War II it was clear to all that the aircraft was dominant over even the greatest of ships.

CHAPTER TWELVE

The End of the Great Ship

With the entry of Italy into the war in 1940, it might have been expected that some action between battlefleets would take place, for the Royal Navy had three based on Alexandria along with several cruisers, and a number of destroyers. It also possessed one great advantage in having an aircraft carrier, *Eagle,* in the Mediterranean fleet. Only a limited number of Gladiator fighters were available for use in fleet protection, but in her offensive role she could carry a number of torpedo bombers. The Italians, on the other hand, had two completely rebuilt and modernized *Conte di Cavour* class 12-inch battleships as well as one or two older ones, and were completing the building of four of the new *Vittorio Veneto* class.

On the only occasion when anything even approaching an action between battleships occurred, the British and Italian fleets were both at sea performing the function for which they were to be used throughout the Mediterranean war — covering convoys in case the enemy should make a battleship attack on them. A flying boat out of Malta first sighted the Italian fleet, consisting of two *Cavour* class battleships, six 8-inch and ten 6-inch gun cruisers, together with thirty-two destroyers, some 145 miles distant from the British fleet. This consisted of that modernized survivor from Jutland, *Warspite,* and the old *Malaya* and *Royal Sovereign,* both slow — the latter notoriously so — together with five 6-inch cruisers, sixteen destroyers, and the aircraft carrier *Eagle.* As the fleets drew together, the British commander-in-chief striving to lay himself between the enemy and Taranto, air reconnaisance on both sides identified their enemy's course and position. Airstrikes were sent out from *Eagle* but failed in their mission. The Italian Admiral Campioni, however, had already wisely decided to make for the security of the Messina Straits, where he could expect air cover from his shore-based air force as well as air attacks to be carried out on the British, who had indeed already been heavily bombed by the Italians during their previous days at sea. (The Mediterranean had been reduced by the aircraft to little more than a lake.)

In the afternoon of that day one of the British cruiser commanders, Captain Rory O'Connor, had the privilege of making the signal 'Enemy battle fleet in sight', for the first time in the Mediterranean since the days of Nelson. Shortly afterwards *Warspite* in the van of the two older British battleships (which were unable to keep up with her) opened fire at 26,000 yards. The Italian battleships replied, both sides shooting well and straddling their targets. Seven minutes after the action began, Admiral Cunningham on *Warspite*'s bridge saw 'the great orange-coloured flash of a heavy explosion at the base of the enemy flagship's funnel'. At the prodigious range of 13 sea miles a direct hit amidships had been scored on the Italian flagship *Giulio Cesare*. With bad damage to her boiler room and 115 casualties she and her companions turned away under cover of thick smoke, and a confused action between destroyers and cruisers followed. This was the only occasion in the long Mediterranean war that the battlefleets ever sighted one another. The Italians wisely refused to be provoked and kept their great ships for the essential threat represented by 'the fleet in being', as well as for a few important convoy duties to their North African colony. Reverting to the role which had first been initiated in this sea in the sixteenth century against Turkish troops at Preveza, the British battleships were used to bombard enemy ports and positions and, in the later phases of the war, to cover allied troop landings. Indeed, the allied landings at Salerno in 1943 (very fiercely contested by the Germans) were, as they themselves later confirmed, only made possible by the immense weight of heavy gunfire from the ships just off the coast. In this capacity alone, the battleships still played an important part throughout World War II, both in the European and Pacific theatres of war.

The real end of the great ship, the heavily armed and armoured, steam turbine-driven successor to the ship of the line, was signalled at Taranto in southern Italy on 11 November 1940. In the summer of that year Admiral Cunningham's fleet at Alexandria had been reinforced by the arrival of the new aircraft carrier HMS *Illustrious*, with her armoured flight deck and a complement of the latest Fulmar fighters as well as Swordfish biplane torpedo bombers, which though slow were most effective. With this great strike potential in his hands Cunningham and his staff began planning a major attack on the Italian main fleet base at Taranto, tucked up in the great gulf that forms the sole of Italy, which had been out of range of air attack up to that moment. The plan was for both *Illustrious* and *Eagle* to be brought unobserved to a flying-off position within range of Taranto. Unfortunately, the old carrier *Eagle* developed serious engine defects caused by the many near misses she had recently received from Italian bombing attacks and had to be withdrawn, leaving *Illustrious* alone as the heart of the operation. This was designed to take place under cover of the passage of a major convoy from Gibraltar through to the eastern Mediterranean, and other activities involving British convoys to Greece and attacks by fleet units against Italian positions in Albania.

Permanent air reconnaissance was being kept over Taranto by RAF planes out of Malta and as *Illustrious*, covered by a battleship and destroyer escort, made for the flying-off position west of Greece, the report came through that the sixth Italian battleship in their fleet had just entered Taranto harbour. As Admiral Cunningham remarked '...all the pheasants had come home to roost'. (Lord Cunningham, *A Sailor's Odyssey*). During the night of 11 November 1940 the attack was launched. Made in two waves of twelve aircraft each, coming in about one hour apart, the attack was a resounding success despite heavy anti-aircraft fire. It changed the balance of power in the Mediterranean and altered the whole course of naval history. Two Italian battleships were sunk and one, hit in the bows, had to be beached; a cruiser and two destroyers were also damaged. 'Taranto and the night of the 11th-12th,' as Admiral Cunningham was to write, 'should be remembered forever as having shown once and for all that in the Fleet Air Arm the Navy has its most devastating weapon.'

This was true, although this 'devastating weapon' depended on the large and relatively unwieldy vessels that carried the aircraft. Inevitably they had their great weakness: fast though they were, they presented large targets. Unlike battleships they could not be constructed with anti-torpedo bulges and, since their great structures were in effect little more than aircraft hangars afloat, they could not be sufficiently compartmentalized. Two of Britain's aircraft carriers fell victim to German U-boat attacks during the course of fleet and convoy protection duties in the Mediterranean and two more, despite their armoured flight decks, were so badly damaged by shore-based divebomber attacks as to be too crippled for further action, requiring many months of repair in distant navy yards. The advent of the efficient German Luftwaffe into the Mediterranean theatre soon made it obvious that in a constricted area, where land-based aircraft could cover almost every part of the sea, the new successor to the battleship was very vulnerable.

That the aircraft carrier proved the dominant ship in the Pacific theatre of war was due to the immense distances involved, distances that were beyond the range of any reconnaissance aircraft available at that time. Once reconnaissance from satellites in space became available in the post-war years it was clear that even the giant nuclear-powered aircraft carriers of the US Navy were no longer secure from detection in any ocean however large. Long before the last quarter of the twentieth century even the Pacific had shrunk to somewhat similar dimensions to the Mediterranean during World War II.

One of the last actions in the Mediterranean in which an Italian battleship, *Vittorio Veneto*, was nearly brought into action by the British fleet out of Alexandria occurred in March 1941. An air strike launched from HMS *Formidable* with torpedo bombers having failed against Admiral Iachino's *Vittorio Veneto*, he and a major part of his fleet had turned away, wisely unwilling to hazard a capital ship in the vicinity of a carrier. In another air strike, however, an Italian heavy cruiser was torpedoed and came to a stop. Unaware that the British had capital ships nearing the area, Admiral Iachino sent back two other cruisers of the same class overnight to stand by their crippled sister ship, and either take off the crew and sink her, or take her in tow. These three in company with escorting destroyers were unlucky enough to be lying directly in the path of the advancing British fleet. Detected first of all by radar (which the Italians still did not have) they were blown to pieces — at almost point blank range for 15-inch guns — while *Vittorio Veneto*, which the British were looking for, escaped at high speed to the west. The fate of these fine 10,000 ton, 8-inch gun cruisers, showed that the Italians had no conception of the possibility of night action. This was revealed by the fact that the main armament on all three of them was unmanned and the guns still trained fore and aft when they were first sighted visually, and within minutes of their destruction. Admiral Cunningham summed up the action off Cape Matapan: 'They had good ships, good guns and torpedoes, flashless ammunition and much else; but even their newest ships lacked the radar which had served us so well, while in the art of night fighting in heavy ships they were no further advanced than we had been at Jutland twenty-five years before.'

Although the carrier-borne aircraft had not succeeded in their most important mission — to damage and reduce the speed of the Italian battleship — it was their crippling of the Italian cruiser that had promoted the final night action. Throughout the whole operation they had enabled Admiral Cunningham to have a fairly accurate picture of the movements of the enemy at sea — something which Admiral Iachino was later to confess that he did not have at all. (After Matapan the Italian dictator ordered the laying down of an aircraft carrier. It was too late, for the Italian surrender took place before any real progress had been made on its construction.)

The Italian battleships in their harbour-bound role continued to exercise their powerful presence and consequently exert a marked effect on British policy, leading to the necessity to keep an aircraft carrier in this theatre and, after the Japanese had entered the war, caused the retention of heavy ships in the Mediterranean which could well have proved useful in the Far East. Similarly, after the sinking of *Bismarck,* the existence of her sister ship *Tirpitz,* tucked away in the fjords of Norway, forced the British always to keep at least two ships of her class capable of dealing with her (for they knew what *Bismarck* had cost), together with an aircraft carrier, in those old northern waters where once the Grand Fleet had been similarly detained.

The Japanese attack on Pearl Harbour in December 1941, although on a greater scale, merely confirmed what Taranto had already demonstrated. (Indeed, in view of the Japanese aptitude for assimilating ideas from the West and improving upon them, the Royal Navy's operation against the Italian fleet may well have provided the original blue print for the destruction of the US Navy's battleship strength.) But Admiral Yamamoto, whose long term outlook on the future of naval warfare was in advance of most, did not see Pearl Harbour as the overwhelming victory that he had hoped for; he was already aware that, especially in the Pacific, the battleship was a thing of the past because the carrier-borne aircraft far outranged the largest naval gun. The fact that the three American aircraft carriers were absent from Pearl Harbour at the time of Yamamoto's attack greatly diminished the victory in his eyes. It was around the kernel of these three ships and a fourth, which at the time was being refitted in the United States, that the Americans were to build their carrier task forces which came to dominate the whole Far East war.

After a first success with carriers, escorted by destroyers and cruisers, in the battle of the Coral Sea, the Americans went on to a victory that was the turning point of the Pacific war. This was the battle of Midway in June 1942, where the action was conducted exclusively by carrier-borne aircraft on both sides. In this new style classic encounter, fought partly at long range, the Japanese lost all four of the aircraft carriers, together with the flower of their aircrews, with which they had entered the conflict. The effect was the same as if, in earlier days, a large part of the battlefleet had been destroyed or, even earlier, the major ships of the line had been lost. The aircraft carrier had now taken their place. Battleships, as has been said, were to be deployed in later stages of the Pacific war when the Americans, 'island-hopping', began to roll back the Japanese-dominated areas of the sea — the domination of which had been first achieved mainly through the deployment of their carriers. There were only two occasions during the Pacific war that battleships of the two sides ever engaged one another. On the first of these, in November 1942, there occurred a night encounter where — as at Matapan — the Americans' use of radar gave them an immense advantage over their Japanese opponents, and resulted in the Japanese battleship *Kirishima* being sunk. In a later battle in the Leyte Gulf two Japanese battleships were literally overwhelmed by a much larger force consisting of six American battleships.

Like ceremonial saluting guns or breastplated cavalry ashore, these great ships continued to be used until the end of World War II as meeting places for the allied leaders (Roosevelt and Churchill in the Atlantic), or as the commander-in-chief's headquarters during seaborne invasions. As the war in both European and Pacific theatres drew to its close, they were also used from the Mediterranean to the Pacific as the imposing symbols of power, aboard which the defeated signed their surrender documents under the eyes of the victors.

The largest battleship ever built in Britain, the last of her line, and the last to be completed throughout the world, was HMS *Vanguard*. She is a footnote to history and little more. Laid down in 1941 with the original intention of her becoming a valuable addition to the naval forces at Singapore, she was overtaken by the outcome of events and work on her consequently slowed down — only being renewed with a view to her adding to the British naval presence in the latter stages of the Pacific war. Again she was overtaken by events, and did not finally complete until 1946. It was fitting, even if far from intended, that the last great battleship or ship of the line should be built in Britain where, in effect, the first had been launched in the reign of King Henry VIII. It was he who had founded the Royal Navy and, in the building of *Great Harry* and *Mary Rose,* had first established that line of 'Great Ships' which was to exercise dominion over seas and oceans for four centuries.

From their first awkwardness, when design and style had not yet adjusted to function, the sailing ship had grown to accommodate the guns that were its *raison d'être* so as to achieve a degree of simple dignity. As in art, there had followed a tendency to elaborate upon this, for little purpose other than to impress and astonish. The Mannerist or Baroque followed upon the Classical. With the great naval wars of the eighteenth century, function had imposed its strict hand upon decoration, leading ultimately to the perfection of the great ship of the line. With steam superseding sail, and wood yielding before iron and steel, again as in art during an age of change and uncertainty, a hotchpotch of design and style ensued. Shipbuilders and sailors were confronted with the confusion caused by the Industrial Revolution. When all things were changing so fast and in so many directions, what is surprising is not perhaps the length of time it took for the new manner to evolve, but how quickly it did so.

As from *Dreadnought* onwards the modern great ship

was to change relatively little in the short half century that remained to her. The age of decoration was long over. But, before her end, the great battleship had evolved a formidable combination of power and beauty that, though it never equalled its sailing predecessors to the same degree, was nevertheless more than just an expression of devastating power alone. It remained for the rocket and the nuclear-powered submarine to impose their concealed presence upon the inhabitants of the world. At the end of it all, now that the long story of the great ship is done, mankind is still looking down the bronze cannon's mouth....

Bibliography

Place of publication London unless otherwise stated

General

BROWNE, D. G., *The Floating Bulwark, 1514-1942* (1963)
FULLER, J. F. C., *The Decisive Battles of the Western World* 3 vols (1953-5)
HALE, J. R., *Famous Sea Fights: Salamis to Jutland* (1939)
IRELAND, Bernard, *Warships* (1978)
LANDSTROM, Björn, *The Ship: A Survey of the History of the Ship* (1961)
MONSON, Sir William, *Naval Tracts* (ed. M. Oppenheim) 5 vols (Naval Record Society, 1902-14)
OPPENHEIM, M., *A History of the Administration of the Royal Navy* (1896)
WILSON, A. W., *The Story of the Gun* (Woolwich 1944)

Oar and Sail

Admiralty Regulations and Instruction, 1790
———   1808
ANDERSON, Roger C., *Lists of Men-of-War,* pt i, 1649-1702 (Society of Nautical Research, Cambridge 1939)
ANDERSON, Roger C. and R., *Sailing Ships* (1947)
ANON., *Life on Board a Man of* War (1829)
BALBI, F., *The Siege of Malta 1565*, trans, from the Spanish (1965)
BARBER, Richard W., *Samuel Pepys Esquire* (1970)
BOUCHER, Lady, *Memoirs of the Life of Admiral Codrington* (1893)

BOXER, C. R., *The Dutch Seaborne Empire., 1600-1800* (2nd ed, 1966)

BRADFORD, E., *The Sultan's Admiral; the Life of Barbarossa* (1969)

_____ *The Story of the 'Mary Rose'* (1982)

_____ *The Great Siege* (1961)

_____ *Drake* (1965)

_____ *Nelson* (1977)

BRENTON, Capt. Edward, *Naval History of Great Britain* (1837 edition)

BRYANT, Arthur, *Pepys: the Saviour of the Navy* (1949)

CALLENDER, Sir Geoffrey, *Portrait of Peter Pett and the Sovereign of the Seas* (Newport, IOW, 1930)

CLOWES, G. S. Laird, *Sailing Ships: Their History and Development,* vols I & II (1932)

CORBETT, Sir Julian, *Drake and the Tudor Navy,* vols I & II (1899)

DEANE, Sir Anthony, *Doctrine of Naval Architecture* (1670)

DRAKE, Sir Francis, *The World Encompassed*, ed. Sir J. C. Temple (Hakluyt Society 1926)

EKINS, Sir Charles, *Naval Battles* (1824) FISHER, Godfrey, *Barbary Legend 1415-1830* (New York 1957)

GEYL, Peter, *The Netherlands in the Seventeenth Century,* 2 vols (1967)

_____ *History of the Low Countries*

_____ *Orange and Stuart* (1969)

GROOT, I de and VOSTMAN, R., *Maritime Prints by the Dutch Masters* (1960)

HARING, Clarence H., *Buccaneers in the West Indies in the 17th Century* (1910)

HUME, Martin, *Spain: Its Greatness and Decay, 1479-1788* (Cambridge 1940)

HUTCHINSON, J. R., *The Press-gang Afloat and Ashore* (1913)

INGRAM, Bruce S. (ed.), *Three Sea Journals of Stuart Times* (1936)

JAMES, William, *Naval History of Great Britain* (1837 edition)

LAUGHTON, Sir John K. (ed.), *State Papers Relating to the Defeat of the Spanish Armada* (Navy Record Society, 1894) LAVERY, B., *The Ship of the Line*, vol I (1983)

LEWIS, Michael, *The Spanish Armada* (1960)

_____ *England's Sea Officers: The Story of the Naval Profession* (1939)

_____ *A Social History of the Navy, 1793-1815* (1960)

MAHAN, A. T., *The Influence of Sea Power in History, 1660-1783(1934:)*

MATTINGLEY, Garrett, *The Defeat of the Spanish Armada* (1959)

McKEE, A., *King Henry VIII's 'Mary Rose'* (1943)

MERRIMAN, R. B., *Suleiman the Magnificent* (Cambridge, Mass., 1944)

PARES, R., *War and Trade in the West Indies, 1739-63* (Oxford 1936)

PEPYS, Samuel, *Diaries*, eds Robert Latham and William Matthews, 11 vols (1970-83)

POOL, Bernard, *Navy Board Contracts 1600-1832* (1966)

POWELL, John, *The Navy in the English Civil War* (Hamden, Conn., 1962)

POWLEY, Edward B., *The English Navy in the Revolution of 1688* (Cambridge 1928)

Public Record Office, Adm. 7/867 Misc., *Progress of the Navy, 1764-1806*

ROWSE, A. L., *The Expansion of Elizabethan England* (1955)

_____ *Sergison Papers*, ed. Merriman (Navy Record Society, 1950)

SOUTHEY, Robert, *The Life of Nelson* (1813)

_____ *Lives of the British Admirals*, 5 vols (1833-40)

TANNER, James R., *Samuel Pepys and the Royal Navy* (Cambridge, 1920)

TREVELYAN, G. M., *England under the Stuarts* (revised ed. 1946)

_____ *England in the Reign of Queen Anne*, 3 vols (1930-4)

TURNER, Francis C., *James II* (1948)

WILLIAMSON, J. A., *The Voyages of the Cabots and the English Discovery of North America under Henry VII and Henry VIII* (1929)

WOODHOUSE, C. M., *The Battle of Navarino* (1965)

Ironclads and Steam

BAGOT, Lt Cmdr W. T., Translation of the German Official Account of Jutland, *Der Krieg zur See 1914-18* (1926)

BARNETT, Correlli, *The Swordbearers: Studies in Supreme Command in the First World War* (1963)

BASSETT, Ronald, *Battle Cruisers* (1981)

BELLAIRS, Carlyon, *The Battle of Jutland: the Sowing and the Reaping* (1920)

BENNETT, G., *The Battle of Jutland* (1964)

BERTHOLD, W., *Sink the 'Bismarck'* (1958)

BRADFORD, E., *The Mighty 'Hood'* (1959)

_____ *Siege: Malta 1940-3* (1985)

BRAGADIN, M. A., *The Italian Navy in World War II* (US Navy Institute, 1957)

BREYERS, S., trans Alfred Kurti, *Battleships and Battle Cruisers, 1905-70* (1973)

BRODIE, B., *Sea Power in the Machine Age* (1941)

CHALMERS, W. S., *Life and Letters of David, Earl Beatty* (1951)

CHATFIELD, Lord, *The Navy and Defence* (1942)

CHURCHILL, W. S., *The World Crisis, 1911-1918* (1923-9)

_____ *The Second World War*, 6 vols (1948-54)

COCCHIA, Admiral (and others), *La Marina Italiana nella Seconda Guerra Mondiale* (Rome 1959)

CORBETT, Sir Julian S., *History of the Great War: Naval Operations*, vols I-III (1921-3)

CUNNINGHAM, Lord, *A Sailor's Odyssey* (1951)

DEWAR, K. G. B., *The Navy from Within* (1939)

DREYER, F., *The Sea Heritage* (1955)

EM IN, Ahmed, *Turkey in the World War* (New Haven, Conn., 1958)

FROST, H., *The Battle of Jutland* (US Naval Institute 1936)

GEORGE, David Lloyd, *War Memoirs* (1933-6)

GOODENOUGH, W., *A Rough Record* (1943)

GROSS, O., see Bagot

HARPER, J. E. T., *The Truth about Jutland* (1927)

HART, B. H. Liddell, *A History of the World War, 1914-18* (1934)

_____ *History of the Second World War* (1970)

HMSO, *The Mediterranean Fleet* (1944)

HODGES, P., *The Big Gun, 1860-1945* (1981)

HURD, A., *The British Fleet in the Great War* (1918) *Jane's Fighting Ships* 1914, 1939

JELLICOE, Earl, *The Grand Fleet, 1914-16* (1919)

_____ *The Crisis of the Naval War* (1920)

_____ *The Submarine Peril* (1934)

KENNEDY, Ludovic, *Menace: The Life and Death of the 'Tirpitz'* (1979)

_____ *Pursuit: The Sinking of the 'Bismarck'* (1974)

KEYES, Sir Roger, *Naval Memoirs* (1934)

KURTI, Alfred, see Breyers, S.

LENTON, H. T., and COLLEDGE, J. J., *Warships of World War II* (1970)

MACINTYRE, D., *Jutland* (1957)

_____ *The Battle for the Mediterranean* (1964)

MARDER, Arthur J., *Fear God and Dread Nought: the Correspondence of Admiral of the Fleet Lord Fisher,* 3 vols (1952-9)

_____ *From Dreadnought to Scapa Flow,* 3 vols (Oxford 1961-6)

_____ *British Naval Policy 1880-1905* (1941)

_____ *Portrait of an Admiral* (1952)

MOOREHEAD, Alan, *Gallipoli* (1956)

NEVINSON, Henry W., *The Dardanelles Campaign* (1918)

NEWBOLT, H., *History of the Great War: Naval Operations,* vols iv-v (1928 & 1931)

OFFICIAL HISTORIES (WORLD WAR I): *Naval Operations* Vol III (1940 edition) and IV
PADFIELD, Peter, *The Battleship Era* (1972)
PAIXHANS, Col., *La Nouvelle Force Maritime* (Paris nd)
PARKES, Oscar, *British Battleships* (1974)
PATTERSON, A. Temple, *Jellicoe* (1969)
PEARS, Randolph, *British Battleships, 1892-1957 (1957)*
PRESTON, A., *Navies of World War II (1976)*
RAVEN, Allen and Roberts, John, *County Class Cruisers* (RSV Publishing Inc, 1978)
ROSKILL, S. W., *HMS Warspite (1957)*
_____ *The War at Sea,* 4 vols (HMSO 1954-61)
_____ *Churchill and the Admirals* (1977)
_____ *Naval Policy between the Wars* (1968)
SCHEER, Adml Reinhard, *Germany's High Seas Fleet in the World* War (1920)
SCHOFIELD, B. B., *Loss of the 'Bismarck'* (1972)
Ship Design, Report of the Committee on, 1905 (HMSO)
TIRPITZ, Grand Adm. von, *My Memoirs* (1919)
Trading in Arms, Report of Royal Commission on, 1936 (HMSO)
WESTWOOD, John N., *The Fighting Ships of World War II* (1973)

About the Author

Ernle Bradford was born in 1922 and died in 1986. He was a noted British historian specializing in the Mediterranean world and naval topics. Bradford was an enthusiastic sailor himself and spent almost thirty years sailing the Mediterranean, where many of his books are set. He served in the Royal Navy during World War II, finishing as the first lieutenant of a destroyer. Bradford lived in Malta for a number of years. He did occasional broadcast work for the BBC, was a magazine editor, and wrote many books, including *Hannibal*, *Paul the Traveller*, *Julius Caesar: The Pursuit of Power*, *Christopher Columbus*, and *The Mighty Hood*.

OPEN ROAD
INTEGRATED MEDIA

Open Road Integrated Media is a digital publisher and multimedia content company. Open Road creates connections between authors and their audiences by marketing its ebooks through a new proprietary online platform, which uses premium video content and social media.

CPSIA information can be obtained
at www.ICGtesting.com
Printed in the USA
JSHW010228110620
6167JS00003B/109